WHAT IS THE BOOK OF JOSHUA?

Kids' Guides to God's Word Series

What Is the Book of Genesis?
What Is the Book of Exodus?
What Is the Book of Leviticus?
What Is the Book of Numbers?
What Is the Book of Deuteronomy?
What Is the Book of Joshua?
What Is the Book of Judges?
What Is the Book of Ruth?
What Is the Book of 1 Samuel?
What Is the Book of 2 Samuel?
What Is the Book of 1 Kings?
What Is the Book of 2 Kings?
What Are the Books of 1–2 Chronicles?
What Are the Books of Ezra & Nehemiah?
What Is the Book of Esther?
What Is the Book of Job?
What Is the Book of Psalms?
What Is the Book of Proverbs?
What Is the Book of Ecclesiastes?
What Are the Books of Song of Songs & Lamentations?
What Is the Book of Isaiah?
What Is the Book of Jeremiah?
What Is the Book of Ezekiel?
What Is the Book of Daniel?
What Are the Books of Hosea–Micah?
What Are the Books of Nahum–Malachi?
What Is the Gospel of Matthew?
What Is the Gospel of Mark?
What Is the Gospel of Luke?
What Is the Gospel of John?
What Is the Book of Acts?
What Is the Book of Romans?
What Is the Book of 1 Corinthians?
What Is the Book of 2 Corinthians?
What Is the Book of Galatians?
What Is the Book of Ephesians?
What Is the Book of Philippians?
What Are the Books of Colossians & Philemon?
What Are the Books of 1–2 Thessalonians?
What Are the Books of 1–2 Timothy & Titus?
What Is the Book of Hebrews?
What Is the Book of James?
What Are the Books of 1–2 Peter & Jude?
What Are the Books of 1-3 John?
What Is the Book of Revelation?

What Is the Book of

JOSHUA?

Michael Whitworth

ISBN 978-1-971767-02-4

Published by Start2Finish
Bend, Oregon 97702
start2finish.org

Printed in the United States of America

30 29 28 27 26 1 2 3 4 5

CONTENTS

INTRODUCTION

Have you ever watched a movie sequel and realized you missed something important? Maybe you jumped into *The Empire Strikes Back* without seeing the original *Star Wars*. Or you started *The Two Towers* without reading *The Fellowship of the Ring*. Suddenly characters are talking about things that happened before, referencing events you never saw, and you're trying to piece together a story that's already in motion.

The book of Joshua is like that. It's not the beginning of the story—it's the continuation of one that's been building for centuries. And if you don't know what came before, you might miss why everything that happens matters so much.

So before we dive in, let's catch up.

THE PROMISE

About five hundred years before Joshua was born, a man named Abraham was living in a place called Ur (modern-day Iraq). God spoke to him with an incredible promise: "Leave your country and go to the land I will show you. I will make you into a great nation."

Abraham obeyed. He packed up everything and traveled to a land called Canaan—the same land where the book of Joshua takes place. When he arrived, God added to his promise: "To your offspring I will give this land."

But here's the thing: Abraham never owned that land. He wandered through it as a foreigner. His son Isaac wandered through it. His grandson Jacob wandered through it. They believed the promise, but they never saw it fulfilled.

Then a famine struck, and Jacob's family—about seventy people—moved to Egypt to survive. They planned to stay temporarily.

They stayed for four hundred years.

SLAVERY AND RESCUE

What started as refuge became slavery. The family of seventy grew into a nation of millions, and the Egyptians forced them into brutal labor. For generations, the Israelites made bricks, built cities, and suffered under Pharaoh's whip.

But God hadn't forgotten his promise.

He raised up Moses—an Israelite who had been raised in Pharaoh's palace but had fled after killing an Egyptian. God appeared to Moses in a burning bush and sent him back to Egypt with a message for Pharaoh: "Let my people go."

Pharaoh refused. God sent ten devastating plagues. Finally, after the death of every firstborn son in Egypt, Pharaoh released the Israelites. They walked out of slavery carrying the wealth of Egypt, and God parted the Red Sea so they could escape Pharaoh's pursuing army.

They were free. The promise was still alive.

THE WILDERNESS

But freedom didn't mean arrival. Between Egypt and the promised land lay a wilderness—and between the Israelites and their inheritance lay their own fear.

When Moses sent twelve spies into Canaan to scout the land, ten of them came back terrified. "The people are giants! The cities are fortified! We can't possibly take that land!"

Only two spies—Joshua and Caleb—trusted God. "We should go up and take possession of the land," they said, "for we can certainly do it." The people sided with the ten. They refused to enter the land.

God's response was severe: that entire generation would die in the wilderness. For forty years, Israel wandered—long enough for everyone who had refused to trust God to pass away. Only Joshua and Caleb, the two faithful spies, would survive to enter the promised land.

A NEW LEADER

As those forty years drew to a close, Moses himself died. He had led Israel out of Egypt, received the Ten Commandments on Mount Sinai, and guided the nation through four decades of wandering. But because of his own failure to honor God at a critical moment, he wasn't allowed to cross into Canaan. He saw the promised land from a mountaintop, and then he died.

The nation needed a new leader. That leader was Joshua.

We don't know a lot about Joshua's early life. We know he was from the tribe of Ephraim, one of the sons of Joseph. We know he had been Moses' assistant for decades, learning leadership by watching the greatest prophet Israel ever had. We know he was one of only two adults from his generation who would actually set foot in the promised land.

And we know that when the book that bears his name begins, he was facing an impossible task: lead a nation of former slaves and wilderness wanderers into a fortified land full of enemies, and somehow take possession of it.

WHAT THIS BOOK IS ABOUT

The book of Joshua tells the story of how God kept his promise. Five hundred years after Abraham first heard that his descendants would inherit the land, Joshua led those descendants across the Jordan River and into Canaan. City by city, battle by battle, the Israelites took possession of what God had sworn to give them.

But this isn't just an ancient war story. It's a book about faith and obedience. It's about what happens when people trust God enough to do what he says, even when it doesn't make sense. It's about the consequences of sin and the power of second chances. It's about how God keeps every single promise he makes. The book divides into three main parts:

Entering the Land (Chapters 1–5): Joshua takes command, sends spies into Jericho, and leads Israel across the Jordan River on dry ground—just as Moses had led them through the Red Sea forty years earlier.

Conquering the Land (Chapters 6–12): The battles begin. Jericho falls when the walls collapse. Ai is conquered after a painful lesson about hidden sin. The southern and northern coalitions are defeated. Thirty-one kings fall before Israel's army—and before Israel's God.

Dividing the Land (Chapters 13–24): With the major battles won, the land is distributed among the twelve tribes. Boundaries are drawn, cities are assigned, and special provisions are made for the Levites and for cities of refuge. The book ends with Joshua's farewell speeches, challenging Israel to choose whom they will serve.

WHY THIS MATTERS

You might wonder why a book written thousands of years ago about ancient battles and land divisions matters today.

Here's why: the book of Joshua shows us what God is like.

He's a God who keeps promises—even when fulfillment takes five hundred years. He's a God who fights for his people when they trust him. He's a God who cares about justice, providing cities of refuge for the innocent and judgment for the guilty. He's a God who gives second chances after failure. He's a God who expects obedience but offers grace when we fall short.

The book also shows us what faith looks like in action. Not faith as a feeling, but faith as a choice—choosing to march around Jericho when it looks ridiculous, choosing to cross a flooded river when there's no bridge, choosing to face giants when you feel like a grasshopper.

And it shows us that choices have consequences. When Israel obeyed, they experienced victory. When they disobeyed—even in hidden ways—they experienced defeat. The book doesn't sugarcoat this. It shows us that God takes sin seriously, even while he offers forgiveness to those who turn back to him.

BEFORE YOU READ

A few things to keep in mind as you work through this book:

The violence is real. The book of Joshua contains some of the most difficult passages in the Bible. God commands the destruction of entire cities. This troubles modern readers—and it should. We'll address this as we go, but know that these weren't random acts of cruelty. They were specific judgments on specific peoples at a specific time, carried out by divine command for reasons the Bible explains.

The geography matters. The book mentions dozens of places—rivers, mountains, cities, valleys. A map can help you visualize what's happening. When Israel marches from Gilgal to Gibeon to Beth Horon, these weren't just names—they were real places where real people walked real miles.

The connections run deep. Almost everything in Joshua connects to something earlier in the Bible. The crossing of the Jordan echoes the crossing of the Red Sea. The fall of Jericho echoes the fall of Egypt. The covenant renewal echoes Mount Sinai. The more you know of the earlier story, the more you'll see in Joshua.

This points forward. For Christians, Joshua points beyond itself to Jesus. In fact, "Joshua" and "Jesus" are the same name in different languages—both mean "The Lord saves." Joshua led God's people into an earthly promised land; Jesus leads his people into an eternal one. Joshua gave Israel rest from their enemies; Jesus offers rest for our souls.

THE ADVENTURE BEGINS

So here we are, standing at the edge of the Jordan River with

Joshua and the Israelites. Behind us: four hundred years of slavery and forty years of wandering. Ahead of us: a land flowing with milk and honey, defended by walled cities and warrior kings.

Moses is dead. The wilderness generation is gone. A new chapter is about to begin.

God's promise to Abraham is about to come true.

Turn the page, and let's watch it happen.

1

THE NEW GUY

In *Spider-Man: Into the Spider-Verse*, Miles Morales is just a regular kid from Brooklyn when everything changes. He gets bitten by a radioactive spider, and suddenly he has powers he doesn't understand and can't control. But here's the really hard part: the original Spider-Man dies. And before he dies, he looks at Miles and basically says, "You have to take over. You have to be Spider-Man now."

Miles is terrified. He's not ready. He can't even control when his hands stick to things. The other Spider-People from different dimensions keep telling him what he needs to hear: "You can do this." But Miles doesn't believe them. He's seen what happened to the last Spider-Man, and he's pretty sure he's about to fail spectacularly.

There's a moment in the movie when Miles is standing on the edge of a building, looking down at the city he's supposed to protect. Everything in him is screaming that he's not enough. The shoes are too big. The responsibility is too heavy. How can he possibly fill the role left by someone so much greater than him?

That's basically where we find Joshua at the beginning of this book. Moses—the greatest leader Israel had ever known—was dead. And Joshua, his assistant, was suddenly standing at the edge of everything God had promised. The Jordan River was in front of him. An entire nation was behind him, waiting for him to lead. And somewhere deep inside, Joshua must have been wondering the same thing Miles wondered: *How am I supposed to do this?*

The book of Joshua is the story of what happened next. It's the story of God's people finally entering the land he had promised them centuries earlier. It's a story of battles and miracles, of faith and failure, of ordinary people caught up in an extraordinary mission.

But more than anything, it's a story about God keeping his promises—even when the people he's working through feel completely inadequate for the job.

WHEN THE GIANT FALLS

To understand why the beginning of Joshua is such a big deal, you need to understand who Moses was.

Moses wasn't just Israel's leader. He was *the* leader. The one God spoke to "face to face, as a man speaks to his friend." The one who stood before Pharaoh and said, "Let my people go." The one who stretched out his staff and watched the Red Sea split in two. The one who climbed Mount Sinai and came down with the Ten Commandments glowing in his hands.

For forty years, Moses had been the constant. The voice of God to the people. The man who interceded when they sinned. The guide through the wilderness. If you were an

Israelite, you literally could not remember a time when Moses wasn't in charge.

And now Moses was dead.

The book of Joshua opens with words that must have sent a chill through the nation: "After the death of Moses..." Think about how that felt. Imagine your whole life, the one leader you've always known suddenly being gone. Imagine standing at the most important moment in your nation's history—finally about to enter the land God promised—and the person who was supposed to lead you there isn't coming.

What do you do when everything depends on someone who just died?

THE VOICE IN THE SILENCE

Here's where the story takes an unexpected turn. In the silence after Moses' death, when everyone was probably wondering what would happen next, God spoke. Not to the elders. Not to the priests. Not to a committee.

God spoke to Joshua. "Moses my servant is dead. Now then, you and all these people, get ready to cross the Jordan River into the land I am about to give to them."

Notice what God didn't say. He didn't say, "I know this is hard. Take some time to grieve. We'll figure this out eventually." He didn't say, "Moses was so great that I'm not sure anyone can replace him." Instead, God said something remarkable: Moses is dead. Now get moving.

This might sound cold, but it's actually incredibly hopeful. God was telling Joshua—and telling us—that his plans don't die with people. His promises don't get buried in tombs. Moses may have seemed irreplaceable as a human being, but God's mission wasn't dependent on Moses. It never had been.

God is the hero of this story. Not Moses. Not Joshua. God. And God was ready to keep going.

THREE TIMES FOR A REASON

What God said next to Joshua is one of the most repeated commands in the whole Bible. Three times in this opening speech, God told Joshua the same thing: "Be strong and courageous."

Why three times? Because Joshua needed to hear it three times. Actually, he probably needed to hear it three hundred times. Taking over for Moses wasn't like taking over your older sibling's lemonade stand. This was leading an entire nation into hostile territory, fighting armies, and claiming land that other people currently occupied.

But here's the crucial thing: God wasn't telling Joshua to psych himself up. He wasn't saying, "Believe in yourself!" or "You've got this!" like some kind of ancient motivational poster.

Look at what God actually said: "Be strong and courageous … for the LORD your God will be with you wherever you go." The command to be brave was connected to a promise of God's presence. Joshua could be strong because God would be with him. Joshua could be courageous because he wasn't going alone. This wasn't about finding inner strength. It was about trusting in someone else's strength entirely.

God also told Joshua something interesting about success: "Keep this Book of the Law always on your lips; meditate on it day and night, so that you may be careful to do everything written in it. Then you will be prosperous and successful."

Wait—the key to military success was reading Scripture? The way to conquer the Promised Land was to study God's Word day and night?

That must have sounded strange. But God knew something Joshua needed to learn: the battles ahead wouldn't be won by superior strategy or bigger armies. They would be won by faithfulness to God. And faithfulness comes from knowing God—knowing his character, his commands, and his promises—through his Word.

THE PEOPLE RESPOND

When Joshua passed along God's instructions to the Israelites, something beautiful happened. The people responded with total support: "Whatever you have commanded us we will do, and wherever you send us we will go. Just as we fully obeyed Moses, so we will obey you. Only may the LORD your God be with you as he was with Moses."

And then they said it too: "Be strong and courageous!" The same words God spoke to Joshua, the people now spoke back to him. It was like an echo of encouragement bouncing between heaven and earth, surrounding Joshua with exactly what he needed to hear.

There's something powerful about that. Joshua wasn't just getting commands from God; he was getting support from his people. Leadership is hard enough when you're alone. But when people rally around you, when they echo God's encouragement back to you, when they commit to follow—that changes everything.

Israel was ready. Joshua was ready. Well, as ready as anyone could be to cross a flooded river and invade a fortified land.

But before the crossing, there was one more thing to do.

THE SPY MISSION

Joshua sent two spies secretly to check out the land, especially the city of Jericho. Jericho was basically the gateway to Canaan—a heavily fortified city that would need to be conquered first. Joshua wanted intelligence. He wanted to know what they were up against.

The spies slipped into the city and ended up at the house of a woman named Rahab. The text tells us directly what she was: a prostitute. Not a temple priestess or a business owner who happened to rent rooms. This is important because it tells us something about the kind of people God works with—but we'll get to that in a minute.

Someone spotted the spies and reported them to the king of Jericho. Soldiers came to Rahab's door demanding she hand them over.

But Rahab had already hidden them on her roof under stalks of flax. She told the soldiers, "Yes, the men came to me, but I didn't know where they came from. They left at dusk when the city gate was about to close. I don't know which way they went. Go after them quickly—you might catch them!" The soldiers rushed off toward the Jordan River, and the city gate was shut behind them.

Now, we need to pause here because some people get really hung up on Rahab's lie. Was it wrong? Was it justified? People have debated this for centuries.

But here's what's interesting: the writer doesn't seem very concerned about the lie. He's not highlighting it or condemning it or praising it. Instead, he rushes right past it to get to what he really wants us to hear—what Rahab said next.

THE CONFESSION THAT CHANGED EVERYTHING

With the soldiers gone and the spies still hidden on her roof, Rahab climbed up to talk with them. And what came out of her mouth was astonishing. "I know that the LORD has given you this land and that a great fear of you has fallen on us, so that all who live in this country are melting in fear because of you. We have heard how the LORD dried up the water of the Red Sea for you when you came out of Egypt, and what you did to the two Amorite kings east of the Jordan. When we heard of it, our hearts melted in fear and everyone's courage failed because of you, for the LORD your God is God in heaven above and on the earth below."

Read that again. A Canaanite prostitute just made one of the most remarkable confessions of faith in the entire Bible. She acknowledged that God had given Israel the land. She recounted God's mighty acts—the Red Sea, the victories over enemy kings. She declared that the people of Jericho were terrified. And then she made a theological statement that most Israelites would have agreed with: "The LORD your God is God in heaven above and on the earth below."

How did Rahab know all this? She heard. News traveled in the ancient world. Stories of what God had done for Israel had spread across the region. Everyone in Jericho had heard the same stories.

But here's the difference: everyone else heard the stories and just felt afraid. Rahab heard the stories and believed. She didn't just feel fear—she felt faith. She realized that if Israel's God could do those things, he must be the true God. And if he was giving Israel the land, she wanted to be on his side.

Faith comes from hearing. Rahab heard about what God had done, and she believed.

THE DEAL

Based on her faith, Rahab made a request: "Now then, please swear to me by the LORD that you will show kindness to my family, because I have shown kindness to you. Give me a sure sign that you will spare the lives of my father and mother, my brothers and sisters, and all who belong to them—and that you will save us from death." She wanted in. She was switching sides. She was betting her life—and her whole family's lives—on Israel's God.

The spies agreed. They made a deal: when Israel attacked the city, Rahab would tie a scarlet cord in her window. Everyone in that house would be spared. But if anyone left the house or if Rahab told anyone about the spies, the deal was off.

Rahab agreed. She lowered the spies down the outside of the city wall by a rope (her house was built right into the wall), and she tied the scarlet cord in her window.

The scarlet cord is one of those details that has fascinated readers for thousands of years. Some people see it as a symbol—the red cord marking a house for salvation, like the blood on the doorposts during the Passover in Egypt. Others see it as simply a practical marker so the Israelite soldiers would know which house to spare.

Either way, the cord represented Rahab's faith made visible. She didn't just believe in her heart; she tied that cord in her window where everyone could see it. Her faith showed up in her actions.

THE REPORT

The spies hid in the hills for three days until the search parties gave up. Then they crossed back over the Jordan and reported to Joshua. Their report was simple and confident: "The LORD has surely given the whole land into our hands; all the people are melting in fear because of us."

Forty years earlier, twelve spies had explored this same land. Ten of them came back terrified, focused on the giants and fortified cities. Only two—Joshua and Caleb—had faith that God would give them victory. That faithless generation died in the wilderness.

Now, a new generation stood at the edge of the same land. And this time, the report was different. The spies had seen firsthand that Jericho was afraid. They had met a woman whose faith proved that God was already at work behind enemy lines. They came back confident not in their own strength but in God's promise.

The way was clear. It was time to cross.

WHAT THIS MEANS FOR US

So what does any of this have to do with your life?

First, God's plans don't depend on any single person. Moses died, but God's mission continued. Whatever you're facing, whatever transition or loss or change has shaken your world, God is still working. He always has the next chapter planned.

Second, courage comes from God's presence, not our own strength. Joshua wasn't told to believe in himself. He was told to trust in God's presence. When you face something scary—a new school, a difficult conversation, a challenge that seems too big—the question isn't, "Am I strong enough?" The question is, "Is God with me?" And the answer is yes.

Third, knowing God's Word matters more than we think. God told Joshua that success would come from meditating on Scripture day and night. That might seem disconnected from conquering cities, but God knew that faithfulness flows from relationship, and relationship grows through his Word. The same is true for us.

Fourth, God works through unlikely people. Rahab was about as far from "respectable religious person" as you could get. But she's the hero of chapter two. She ends up in the genealogy of Jesus himself. God delights in working through people nobody would choose, people the world overlooks, people with messy pasts and complicated stories.

Fifth, faith shows up in action. Rahab didn't just believe in her heart. She hid the spies, lied to the soldiers, made a deal, and tied a cord in her window. Her faith moved her feet and her hands. Real faith always does.

TALKING POINTS

Here are some things to think about and discuss:

1. **Joshua had to step into a role that seemed way too big for him.** Have you ever been in a situation where you felt completely inadequate for what you had to do? What happened?

2. **God told Joshua to be "strong and courageous" three**

times. Why do you think he repeated it? What does it tell us about Joshua—and about ourselves—that we need to hear encouragement over and over?

3. **Rahab heard the same stories about God that everyone else in Jericho heard, but she responded differently.** What made the difference? Why do some people hear about God and believe while others hear and just feel afraid?

4. **Rahab had a pretty sketchy past, yet God used her in an important way.** What does this tell us about the kinds of people God is willing to work with? Does it change how you think about yourself or others?

5. **The spies' report was completely different from the fearful report forty years earlier.** What had changed? What does this teach us about the relationship between faith and how we see our circumstances?

The spies were back. The report was in. The people of Jericho were melting in fear, and a scarlet cord hung in a window on the city wall.

Everything was set. The promises made to Abraham centuries ago were about to become reality. The land that had been waiting for God's people was finally within reach.

But first, they had to cross an uncrossable river.

Turn the page.

2

THE IMPOSSIBLE RIVER

In *The Prince of Egypt*, there's a moment that gives you chills every time you watch it. The Israelites are trapped. The Egyptian army is thundering toward them from behind—chariots, horses, and soldiers with spears. In front of them is the Red Sea, stretching endlessly to the horizon. There's nowhere to go. The people are screaming and panicking, convinced they're about to die.

And then Moses raises his staff.

The wind begins to blow. The waters start to move. And slowly, impossibly, a path opens through the sea. Walls of water rise up on either side as the Israelites walk through on dry ground.

It's one of the most dramatic moments in the whole Bible—and in the movie, you can feel the weight of it. This wasn't supposed to happen. Water doesn't do that. But God did it anyway, because nothing is impossible for him.

Now here's the thing: the generation that walked through the Red Sea never made it to the Promised Land. They died in the wilderness because they refused to trust God. But their children—the generation standing at the edge of the Jordan River in Joshua 3—they grew up hearing stories about what happened at the Red Sea. They knew what God could do.

And now God was about to do it again.

The Jordan River was at flood stage. It was spring, harvest time, and the river had swollen to a raging torrent—maybe a mile wide in places, covering the entire floodplain with swirling, muddy water. This wasn't a gentle stream you could wade across. This was a barrier. An obstacle. An impossibility.

And God said, "Cross it."

THE WAITING GAME

Have you ever had to wait for something big to happen, and the waiting felt almost unbearable? Maybe you were waiting for tryout results. Or for your parents to tell you whether you could go on the trip. Or for a doctor to come back with news. The minutes felt like hours. You couldn't think about anything else.

That's where Israel was in Joshua 3. They had moved from Shittim (where the spies had returned with their report) to the edge of the Jordan. And then they waited. Three days.

Three days of staring at an uncrossable river.

Three days of knowing God had promised them the land on the other side.

Three days of wondering how in the world this was going to work.

The text doesn't tell us what they talked about during those three days, but I imagine the conversations were intense. Some people probably told stories about the Red Sea. Others probably voiced their doubts—"But that was Moses. This is Joshua.

Is he really up for this?"

Why did God make them wait? We don't know for certain, but delays often serve a purpose. Maybe God wanted the impossibility of the situation to sink in. Maybe he wanted them to feel the weight of their helplessness so that when deliverance came, there would be no doubt about who deserved the credit.

God often works that way. He brings us to the end of ourselves before he shows us his power.

THE ARK GOES FIRST

On the third day, the officers went through the camp with instructions: "When you see the ark of the covenant of the LORD your God, and the Levitical priests carrying it, you are to move out from your positions and follow it."

The ark of the covenant was the most sacred object Israel possessed. It was a gold-covered wooden chest that contained the tablets of the Ten Commandments. More importantly, it represented God's presence among his people. Wherever the ark went, God was leading.

And God was about to lead them straight into an impossible river.

The instructions continued: "Keep a distance of about a thousand yards between you and the ark; do not go near it. Then you will know which way to go, since you have never been this way before."

A thousand yards is about half a mile. Why so far back? Partly because the ark was holy—you didn't just crowd around God's presence casually. But there was also a practical reason. If everyone stayed a half mile back, they could all see what was happening at the front. They could all witness whatever God was about to do. This wasn't going to be a private miracle. It was going to be a public display of power that everyone would see.

Joshua added his own instruction: "Consecrate yourselves, for tomorrow the LORD will do amazing things among you." Consecrate yourself. Set yourself apart. Prepare. In ancient Israel, this meant washing your clothes, confessing your sins, and focusing your heart on God. It was like the difference between casually scrolling through your phone and putting everything away because something important is about to happen.

God was about to do "amazing things"—the kind of things that would leave them astonished. But to appreciate what God was doing, they needed to be ready to see it.

THE PROMISE TO JOSHUA

Before the crossing, God spoke privately to Joshua. And what God said must have been exactly what Joshua needed to hear. "Today I will begin to exalt you in the eyes of all Israel, so they may know that I am with you as I was with Moses."

Remember, Joshua was still the new guy. Moses had been the leader for forty years. Joshua had only been in charge for a few days. Some people were probably still wondering if he was the right choice. Could he really fill Moses' sandals?

God's answer was clear: "I will show them. I will do something so unmistakably powerful that everyone will know I am with you."

The miracle at the Jordan wasn't just about getting across a river. It was about confirming Joshua's leadership. It was about showing Israel that the same God who worked through Moses was now working through Joshua. The methods might look different, but the power was the same.

Then God gave Joshua the specific instructions. He was to tell the priests carrying the ark to walk into the Jordan and stand in the river.

That's it. Walk in and stand there. No splitting the waters first. No waiting for the river to dry up. Just walk into the flood and stand there.

Think about how much faith that required. The priests would be carrying the most sacred object in Israel straight into a raging current. If nothing happened, they would be swept away.

THE SETUP

Joshua gathered the people and made an announcement. "Come here and listen to the words of the LORD your God." He wanted their full attention. What he was about to say would change everything. "This is how you will know that the living God is among you and that he will certainly drive out before you the Canaanites, Hittites, Hivites, Perizzites, Girgashites, Amorites and Jebusites."

Seven nations. Seven peoples who currently occupied the land God had promised to Israel. Joshua was telling them, "You're worried about crossing the river? The river is just the beginning. God is going to drive out entire nations for you. And what happens today will prove it."

Then came the key instruction: "See, the ark of the covenant of the Lord of all the earth will go into the Jordan ahead of you. Now then, choose twelve men from the tribes of Israel, one from each tribe. And as soon as the priests who carry the ark of the LORD—the Lord of all the earth—set foot in the Jordan, its waters flowing downstream will be cut off and stand up in a heap."

Did you catch that title? "The Lord of all the earth." Not just the Lord of Israel. Not just a tribal god who had power in one region. The Lord of all the earth. The God who made the rivers could certainly stop one whenever he wanted.

The priests' feet would touch the water, and the water would stop flowing.

It was a promise. Now they had to see if it would happen.

THE MOMENT

The writer slows down here because he wants us to feel the tension. "Now the Jordan is at flood stage all during harvest."

There it is—the detail that makes everything more intense. This wasn't just a river. It was a river at its worst. The banks had overflowed. The current was powerful. Anyone looking at the Jordan that day would have said crossing was impossible.

God loves impossible situations. They're his specialty.

"Yet as soon as the priests who carried the ark reached the Jordan and their feet touched the water's edge, the water from upstream stopped flowing." The priests walked forward. Their feet touched the water. And everything changed.

Somewhere upstream, near a town called Adam, the water stopped. The text says it "piled up in a heap a great distance away." The flow just … stopped. The water that had been rushing toward them backed up and held.

And the riverbed in front of them went dry. "The priests who carried the ark of the covenant of the LORD stopped in the middle of the Jordan and stood on dry ground, while all Israel passed by until the whole nation had completed the crossing on dry ground."

Picture it. The priests standing in the middle of what had been a flooded river, holding the ark, not moving. And on either side of them, thousands and thousands of people walking past on ground that had been underwater just moments before.

Families with children. Older people who remembered the wilderness. Young warriors ready to fight. All of them walking on dry ground through the middle of the Jordan River.

It was impossible. And it happened anyway.

THE TWELVE STONES

While the people were still crossing, God gave Joshua another instruction. "Choose twelve men from among the people, one from each tribe, and tell them to take up twelve stones from the middle of the Jordan, from right where the priests are standing, and carry them over with you and put them down at the place where you stay tonight." Twelve men. Twelve stones. One for each tribe of Israel.

This wasn't random. God wasn't just interested in the miracle—he was interested in the memory. He wanted Israel to remember what happened here. Not just the generation that crossed, but also their children. And their children's children.

Joshua explained the purpose: "In the future, when your children ask you, 'What do these stones mean?' tell them that the flow of the Jordan was cut off before the ark of the covenant of the LORD. When it crossed the Jordan, the waters of the Jordan were cut off. These stones are to be a memorial to the people of Israel forever." A memorial. A reminder. A pile of rocks that would make curious kids ask questions.

"Dad, what are those stones for?"

"Let me tell you a story about the day we crossed the Jordan…"

God knows something important about human beings: we forget. We forget quickly. We forget the most amazing things. Something miraculous happens, and a year later we're living like it never occurred. We need reminders.

The twelve stones at Gilgal (the place where Israel camped after the crossing) were meant to be conversation starters. Every time an Israelite family walked past them, kids would ask questions. And parents would tell the story. Generation after generation would hear about the day God stopped the river.

THE CROSSING COMPLETE

Once everyone had crossed, Joshua gave the final command. The priests carrying the ark walked up out of the riverbed onto the western bank. "And as soon as the priests who carried the ark of the covenant of the LORD came up out of the Jordan and their feet touched dry ground, the waters of the Jordan returned to their place and flooded over all its banks as before."

The timing was unmistakable. The moment the priests' feet left the riverbed, the water came rushing back. This was God's work, pure and simple.

Israel was across. Every single person. Every animal. Every

piece of baggage.

They had entered the Promised Land.

THE DATE THAT MATTERS

The writer includes a small detail that's easy to miss: "On the tenth day of the first month the people went up from the Jordan and camped at Gilgal."

Why does that date matter? Because the tenth day of the first month was the exact day, forty years earlier, when Israel had begun preparing to leave Egypt. It was the day they selected their Passover lambs before the final plague. The day their redemption started.

Now, on that same date, their redemption was reaching its next great milestone. What God began forty years ago, he was now bringing to completion. The slaves who left Egypt were becoming the heirs who entered the Promised Land.

God writes his faithfulness across the calendar.

THE LESSON JOSHUA PREACHED

Joshua gathered the people and made sure they understood what had just happened. This wasn't just a convenient river crossing. This was a message—to Israel and to the watching world. "He did this so that all the peoples of the earth might know that the hand of the LORD is powerful and so that you might always fear the LORD your God." Two audiences. Two purposes.

For the nations—for the Canaanites watching from the other side, for the kings who would hear about this event—the message was clear: Israel's God is powerful. What he did at the

Red Sea forty years ago, he can do again. You cannot stop him.

For Israel—for the people who had just walked through on dry ground—the message was equally clear: Fear the Lord. Not terror, but reverent awe. The kind of deep respect that comes from seeing God's power up close. The kind of trust that says, "If God can do this, he can do anything. I will follow him."

The chapter ends with a report on how the message landed: "Now when all the Amorite kings west of the Jordan and all the Canaanite kings along the coast heard how the LORD had dried up the Jordan before the Israelites until they had crossed over, their hearts melted in fear and they no longer had the courage to face the Israelites."

Rahab had told the spies that the people of Jericho were already afraid. Now that fear had spread to every king in the land. Before Israel fought a single battle, their enemies were already defeated in their hearts.

God had crossed his people over. And everyone knew it.

WHAT THIS MEANS FOR US

So what does an ancient river crossing have to do with your life?

First, God specializes in impossible situations. The Jordan at flood stage wasn't an accident. God didn't say, "Wait until summer when the water's lower." He said, "Cross now, when it looks impossible." He delights in showing his power precisely when we have no power of our own. If you're facing something that looks impossible, that might be exactly where God wants to work.

Second, faith often means stepping in before you see results. The priests didn't wait for the water to stop before they walked in. They walked in, and then the water stopped. Faith isn't waiting until everything makes sense. Faith is trusting God's promise and taking the next step, even when you can't see how it will work out.

Third, we need reminders. God knew Israel would forget. So he gave them stones. We forget too. That's why we have Scripture. That's why we have the Lord's Supper. That's why we tell stories of what God has done. We need tangible reminders because our memories are short and our faith is fragile.

Fourth, God's work has witnesses in mind. The Jordan miracle wasn't private. Everyone saw it—Israel and their enemies. When God works in your life, it's not just for you. It's so others can see and know that he is real.

Fifth, what God starts, he finishes. Forty years passed between the Red Sea and the Jordan. An entire generation died in the wilderness. But God's promise didn't die with them. What he began, he completed. If God has started something in your life, he will finish it. The timeline might be longer than you expect, but his faithfulness doesn't have an expiration date.

TALKING POINTS

Here are some things to think about and discuss:

1. **God made Israel wait three days at the edge of the river before crossing.** Why do you think God makes us wait sometimes? What might be the purpose of delays in our lives?

2. **The priests had to step into the water before it stopped flowing.** Can you think of times when faith required action before you could see results? What makes that kind of faith so hard?

3. **God told Israel to set up memorial stones so future generations would ask questions and hear the story.** What are some "memorial stones" in your own life—reminders of what God has done? How do you make sure you don't forget?

4. **The miracle at the Jordan was partly to confirm Joshua's leadership.** How does it help us when God publicly shows that he's with someone? How does it affect our willingness to follow leaders?

5. **The kings of Canaan "melted in fear" when they heard what happened.** Why do you think hearing about God's power affected them that way? What does it take for someone to move from fear to faith, like Rahab did?

The water was back. The Jordan flowed on as if nothing had happened. But everything had changed. Israel was in the land. The promises made to Abraham were becoming reality. The Canaanite kings were trembling. And at Gilgal, twelve stones stood in a pile—silent witnesses to a day when God stopped a river. The crossing was complete. But the conquest was just beginning.

Turn the page.

3

THE STRANGEST BATTLE PLAN EVER

In *The Karate Kid*, there's a moment that makes absolutely no sense—until it does. Daniel wants to learn karate. He needs to learn karate. There's a bully named Johnny who keeps beating him up, and Daniel is desperate for Mr. Miyagi to teach him how to fight back. But instead of teaching him punches and kicks, Mr. Miyagi hands him a sponge and points to a bunch of cars.

"Wax on. Wax off."

Daniel spends hours waxing cars. Then he paints fences. Then he sands decks. Day after day of what looks like pointless chores while the tournament gets closer and closer. Daniel gets frustrated. He gets angry. He's about to quit when Mr. Miyagi finally shows him the truth: every single motion—wax on, wax off, paint the fence, sand the floor—was actually training his muscles to block attacks. What looked like wasted time was actually essential preparation.

Joshua 5–6 works the same way. Israel had just crossed the Jordan River. Jericho was right there—a fortified city standing between them and the land God had promised. Every military instinct would say: attack now while the enemy is terrified. Strike while the iron is hot. Don't give them time to recover. But God said, "Not yet. First, there's something more important."

What followed was a series of events that must have seemed as strange to Israel as waxing cars seemed to Daniel. Rituals. Ceremonies. Waiting. And then, when it was finally time to take Jericho, God gave them a battle plan that made no military sense whatsoever.

But God knew exactly what he was doing.

THE PAUSE BUTTON

Picture the scene: Israel is camped at Gilgal, just a few miles from Jericho. The city is locked up tight—gates barred, nobody going in or out. The people of Jericho are terrified. News of the Jordan River miracle has spread, and they know they're next.

This would be the perfect time to attack, right?

Instead, God told Joshua to circumcise all the men of Israel.

Now, we need to understand what this meant. Circumcision was the sign of God's covenant with Abraham, going all the way back to Genesis 17. Every male in Israel was supposed to be circumcised as a baby. It marked them as belonging to God's people.

But here's the problem: an entire generation had grown up in the wilderness without being circumcised. The men who had left Egypt as adults had the sign of the covenant, but they had also refused to trust God. They had seen the Promised Land from a distance and said, "We can't do it. The people there are too strong." Because of their unbelief, that whole generation died in the wilderness over forty years.

Their children—the ones now standing at Gilgal—had been born during those wilderness years. And for reasons the text doesn't fully explain, they had never received the covenant sign. They were God's people, but they didn't bear the mark that said so. Before Israel could move forward, this had to be fixed.

So Joshua obeyed. Every man in Israel was circumcised at a place they named Gibeath Haaraloth. And then they had to wait—because after circumcision, you can't exactly go into battle. The men needed time to heal.

Think about how vulnerable Israel was during this time. Their entire fighting force was out of commission. If Jericho had attacked, it would have been a disaster. But God's timing was perfect. The people of Jericho were too paralyzed with fear to do anything. While Israel was at their weakest physically, their enemies were at their weakest mentally. God had it all figured out.

When the healing was complete, God said something significant: "Today I have rolled away the reproach of Egypt from you." The shame was gone. The forty years of wandering—God's discipline on the previous generation—was officially over. This new generation was ready. They bore the mark of the covenant. They belonged to God. And now they could move forward.

THE LAST MANNA, THE FIRST GRAIN

Something else happened at Gilgal that might seem small but was actually huge. Israel celebrated the Passover. This was the festival that commemorated their rescue from Egypt—the night when the angel of death passed over the houses marked with lamb's blood. They had celebrated it in Egypt at the beginning of their journey. Now they celebrated it in Canaan, near the end. And the day after Passover, they ate food from the land—unleavened bread and roasted grain from the produce of Canaan.

That same day, the manna stopped.

For forty years, God had fed Israel with manna—mysterious bread that appeared on the ground every morning. It was supernatural provision. They were in the wilderness where nothing grew, so God made food fall from the sky. But now they were in the land. Now there was grain in the ground and fruit on the trees. They didn't need miraculous bread anymore because ordinary bread was available.

Does that mean God stopped providing for them? Not at all. The grain that grew in Canaan was just as much God's provision as the manna that fell from heaven. It just came through ordinary means instead of extraordinary ones.

Here's something worth thinking about: we often only notice God's provision when it's dramatic. We thank him for the miracle but forget to thank him for the normal stuff—the paycheck, the meal, the safe drive home. But God is behind all of it. Manna in the wilderness and grain in Canaan are both gifts from the same generous Father.

THE COMMANDER

Then came one of the strangest encounters in the whole book. Joshua was near Jericho, probably scouting the city, thinking about how in the world they were going to take it down. Jericho was a fortress. Its walls were thick and tall. Israel had no siege equipment, no battering rams, no experience with this kind of warfare.

And then Joshua looked up and saw a man standing in front of him with a drawn sword. Joshua, being a soldier, asked the obvious question: "Are you for us or for our enemies?" The answer was unexpected: "Neither. I have come as commander of the army of the LORD." Wait—neither? Joshua wanted to know whose side this warrior was on, and the answer was basically: "That's the wrong question."

Joshua immediately realized who he was talking to. He fell facedown and asked, "What does my Lord say to his servant?" The commander's response? "Take off your sandals, for the place where you are standing is holy."

If that sounds familiar, it should. God said the exact same thing to Moses at the burning bush. This wasn't just an angel. This was God himself, appearing as a warrior to lead his people into battle.

And here's the important thing: the commander didn't come to take sides. He came to take over. The question wasn't whether God would join Israel's army. The question was whether Israel would join God's army. There's a big difference.

Sometimes we pray like we're trying to recruit God for our plans. We want him on our team, supporting our agenda. But that's backwards. God is the commander. We're the ones who need to fall in line with his plans. Joshua got it. He took off his sandals and listened.

THE RIDICULOUS PLAN

Now comes the battle plan—and it's one of the strangest

military strategies in history. God told Joshua exactly what to do: March around the city once a day for six days. The armed men go first. Then seven priests carrying trumpets made of ram's horns. Then the ark of the covenant. Then more soldiers bringing up the rear. The priests blow the trumpets, but nobody else makes a sound. No shouting. No war cries. Just marching and trumpet blowing. On the seventh day, march around the city seven times. After the seventh lap, the priests blow a long blast on the trumpets, and then—only then—everyone shouts. And the walls will fall down.

That's it. That's the plan.

Can you imagine being an Israelite soldier and hearing this? You've been training for battle your whole life. You're ready to fight. And the commander tells you to... walk in circles?

Or imagine being a citizen of Jericho, watching from the walls. Day one: the Israelites march around once and leave. Weird, but whatever. Day two: same thing. Day three, four, five, six: same thing. By now you're probably starting to relax. Maybe these people are crazy. Maybe they don't actually know how to attack a city. Maybe we're safe after all.

And then day seven comes.

THE WALLS COME DOWN

On the seventh day, Israel got up at dawn. They marched around the city—not once, but seven times. The only sound was the steady blast of the ram's horn trumpets. After the seventh circuit, Joshua gave the command: "Shout! For the LORD has given you the city!" The people shouted. The trumpets blasted. And the walls of Jericho collapsed.

The text says the walls "fell down flat." Archaeologists have debated exactly what this looked like, but the effect is clear: what had been an impenetrable barrier was suddenly gone. The Israelites charged straight in.

Notice who gets the credit. Israel didn't knock down the walls with battering rams. They didn't tunnel underneath or scale over with ladders. They marched and shouted. That's it. The walls fell because God knocked them down.

This was the point of the strange battle plan. If Israel had taken Jericho by conventional military tactics, they might have congratulated themselves on their brilliant strategy or their fighting skill. But there was no way to look at this victory and think Israel had done it themselves. Walking in circles doesn't knock down walls. Only God does that.

The ark of the covenant was at the center of the procession for a reason. This was God's victory, accomplished by God's presence, for God's glory. Israel participated—they had to march, they had to shout, and they had to obey—but the power was entirely God's.

RAHAB REMEMBERED

In the middle of the destruction, there was rescue.

Remember Rahab? The woman who had hidden the spies and made them promise to save her family? The one who had tied a scarlet cord in her window as a sign? Joshua hadn't forgotten. He sent the two spies—the same men Rahab had protected—to bring her out. They went to her house, found her and her entire family gathered inside, and brought them to safety outside the Israelite camp.

Think about the contrast. Jericho was being destroyed. Everything in it was being devoted to God—given over completely, never to be used again. The city would be burned. No one would be allowed to rebuild it. But in the middle of judgment, there was salvation. One family, because they believed and acted on their belief, was rescued from the destruction falling all around them. The scarlet cord in the window was like the blood on the doorposts in Egypt. Both were signs that said, "This household trusts in God's promise. Pass over us." And God honored both signs.

Rahab didn't just survive. She was brought into the community of Israel. She lived among God's people for the rest of her life. And centuries later, her name would show up in the genealogy of Jesus himself.

That's grace. A Canaanite prostitute becomes an ancestor of the Messiah because she believed.

THE WARNING

But the story of Jericho came with a warning that would prove crucial in the next chapter. Joshua told the people: everything in this city belongs to God. The silver, the gold, the bronze, the iron—it all goes into the Lord's treasury. Don't take anything for yourself. If you do, you'll bring disaster on the whole camp. This was called "the ban" or "the devoted things." The idea was that Jericho, as the first city conquered, was like the firstfruits of the harvest—it belonged entirely to God. Taking anything from it would be stealing from God himself.

The writer of Joshua inserts this warning right at the climax of the story, between Joshua's command to shout and the people's actual shout. He does this because what Joshua says here is actually more important than the walls falling down. Obedience matters more than victory.

We'll see why in the next chapter, when someone ignores this warning and everything falls apart.

WHAT THIS MEANS FOR US

So what does any of this have to do with your life?

First, preparation matters more than we think. Israel couldn't rush into battle. They had to stop, deal with their covenant relationship with God, and get their spiritual house in order before they could move forward. Sometimes God slows us down for reasons we don't understand, and those pauses turn out to be essential.

Second, God provides in different ways at different times. Manna in the wilderness, grain in Canaan—both are God's gifts. Don't only look for God in the miraculous. Learn to see his hand in the ordinary.

Third, the right question isn't "Is God on my side?" but "Am I on God's side?" The commander of the LORD's army didn't come to join Israel's cause. He came to lead. Our job is to fall in line with his plans, not recruit him for ours.

Fourth, God's methods often don't make sense to us. Marching around a city doesn't knock down walls—except when God says it will. Faith means obeying even when the instructions seem ridiculous. Sometimes God works in strange ways specifically so we can't take credit for the results.

Fifth, in the middle of judgment, God makes a way of rescue. Rahab's story shows that no one is too far gone. Anyone who believes and acts on that belief can be saved—no matter their past, their nationality, or their reputation.

TALKING POINTS

Here are some things to think about and discuss:

1. **Israel's first act in the Promised Land was circumcising all the men, leaving the entire army vulnerable for days.** Why do you think God made Israel wait and go through the circumcision ceremony before attacking Jericho? What might have happened if they had rushed ahead without dealing with their covenant relationship first?
2. **The manna stopped when Israel entered the land.** Have you ever experienced God providing for you in one way for a while, and then the provision changing? How did that feel?
3. **The commander said "Neither" when Joshua asked whose side he was on.** Why is that answer so important? How does it change the way we should think about asking God to help us?
4. **The battle plan for Jericho made no military sense.** Why do you think God chose such a strange strategy? What would have been different if Israel had conquered the city through normal fighting?
5. **Rahab was saved because she believed and acted on her belief.** What does her story teach us about faith? About who can be saved?

The walls were down. The city was conquered. Rahab and her family were safe among God's people.

Israel had won their first battle in the Promised Land—not

by their own strength or strategy, but by simple obedience to a God whose plans don't always make sense but always work.

But the warning about the devoted things was still echoing. Would everyone obey?

Turn the page.

4

THE HIDDEN THING

In *Frozen*, there's a moment that changes everything—and not in a good way. Elsa has been hiding her ice powers for years. She's terrified that if anyone finds out, something terrible will happen. So she keeps her secret buried deep, pretending everything is fine, hoping nobody will ever discover the truth.

But secrets have a way of coming out. At her coronation, in a moment of stress, Elsa's powers explode into the open. And suddenly the whole kingdom is affected. Arendelle is plunged into an eternal winter. People are freezing. Anna nearly dies. All because of something hidden.

Elsa's secret wasn't exactly the same as sin—she didn't choose to have ice powers. But the pattern is familiar: something concealed, something buried, something that one person thinks they can keep private... until it affects everyone around them.

That's what happens in Joshua 7. Israel had just experienced an incredible victory at Jericho. The walls fell flat. The city was conquered. God had proven himself powerful beyond anything they could have imagined. Everything seemed set for an easy march through the Promised Land.

But there was something hidden in the camp. One man had done something in secret that he thought no one would ever discover. And because of that hidden thing, everything fell apart.

THE MAN WHO THOUGHT NO ONE WAS WATCHING

His name was Achan. He was from the tribe of Judah—one of Israel's most important tribes. He had marched around Jericho with everyone else. He had shouted when Joshua gave the command. He had watched the walls collapse. And then, in the chaos of victory, Achan saw something he wanted.

Remember the warning from the last chapter? Joshua had told the people that everything in Jericho was "devoted" to God—it all belonged to him. The silver, gold, bronze, and iron were to go into the Lord's treasury. Nobody was to take anything for themselves. If they did, they would bring disaster on the whole camp.

Achan heard that warning. And he ignored it.

Here's how he described it later: "When I saw in the plunder a beautiful robe from Babylonia, two hundred shekels of silver and a bar of gold weighing fifty shekels, I coveted them and took them."

I saw. I coveted. I took.

Sound familiar? It should. It's the same pattern from the garden of Eden, when Eve "saw that the fruit of the tree was good" and "took some and ate it." It's the pattern of temptation that has brought down human beings since the beginning.

Achan dug a hole in the ground under his tent and buried his stolen treasure. He covered it up. He went about his business like nothing had happened. Maybe he convinced himself it wasn't a big deal. Maybe he told himself that nobody would miss a few items from an entire city's worth of plunder. Maybe he thought God wouldn't notice or wouldn't care.

He was wrong.

THE DISASTER AT AI

After Jericho, Israel turned their attention to a smaller city called Ai. Joshua sent spies to check it out, and they came back with a confident report: "Don't bother sending the whole army. This place is small. Two or three thousand men should be plenty."

Notice something missing from that report? Any mention of God. Any reference to the Lord's guidance. Any seeking of divine direction.

At Jericho, the spies had come back talking about how the Lord had given the land into Israel's hands. At Ai, the spies talked only about military calculations—how many men they would need, how easy the victory would be.

Israel had gotten overconfident. They had started thinking victory was automatic. They had stopped depending on God.

About three thousand Israelite soldiers marched up to attack Ai. And they got crushed.

The men of Ai chased them away from the city gates, pursued them down the slopes, and killed thirty-six of them. Thirty-six doesn't sound like a huge number, but this was the first time any Israelites had died in battle since they crossed the

Jordan. After Jericho, they thought they were invincible. Now they were running for their lives. The text says that "the hearts of the people melted in fear and became like water."

Wait—that phrase sounds familiar. Earlier in Joshua, we heard that the hearts of the Canaanites were melting in fear because of Israel. Now Israel's hearts are melting. The roles have reversed. The people who were supposed to be conquering are now the ones who are terrified.

What happened? God wasn't with them anymore. Because of Achan's hidden sin, God had withdrawn his presence from the battlefield. Without God, Israel was just another small nation trying to conquer fortified cities. Without God, they didn't stand a chance.

JOSHUA FALLS APART

When Joshua heard about the defeat, he completely fell apart. He tore his clothes—a sign of grief and distress in ancient times. He fell facedown on the ground in front of the ark of the covenant and stayed there until evening. The elders of Israel joined him, throwing dust on their heads.

And then Joshua prayed, "Alas, Sovereign LORD, why did you ever bring this people across the Jordan to deliver us into the hands of the Amorites to destroy us? If only we had been content to stay on the other side of the Jordan!" Joshua was basically saying, "Why did we even come here? We should have stayed where we were safe!"

He went on: "O Lord, what can I say, now that Israel has been routed by its enemies? The Canaanites and all the other people of the country will hear about this and surround us and wipe out our name from the earth. What then will you do for your own great name?"

There's something interesting in that last question. Joshua wasn't just worried about Israel—he was worried about God's reputation. If Israel got wiped out, what would the nations think about Israel's God? Joshua cared about God's honor, even in his despair.

But notice what Joshua didn't do: he didn't ask if there was sin in the camp. He didn't consider that the problem might be on Israel's side. He assumed God had abandoned them for no reason.

GOD SETS THE RECORD STRAIGHT

God's response was blunt: "Stand up! What are you doing down on your face? Israel has sinned." No gentle sympathy. No "I understand you're having a hard time." Just a direct command to get up and face the truth.

Then God laid out exactly what had happened: "They have violated my covenant, which I commanded them to keep. They have taken some of the devoted things; they have stolen, they have lied, they have put them with their own possessions."

Notice the pronouns. God said "they" and "Israel"—not "he" and "Achan." One man sinned, but God held the whole nation responsible. This is hard for us to understand because we're so individualistic. We think, "That's not fair! Why should everyone suffer for what one person did?"

But Israel wasn't just a collection of individuals—they were a community bound together by covenant. When one member broke faith with God, the whole community was affected. It's like a sports team: if one player cheats, the whole team might have to forfeit their wins. If one member of a family does something wrong, the whole family feels the shame.

God told Joshua what had to be done. The next morning, Israel would gather tribe by tribe. God would identify the guilty party through a process of elimination—first the tribe, then the clan, then the family, then the individual. The person found guilty would be destroyed along with everything he had. The hidden thing would be brought into the light.

THE UNVEILING

The next morning, Joshua assembled Israel. The process began.

Tribe by tribe, they came forward. The tribe of Judah was taken.

Clan by clan within Judah. The Zerahite clan was taken.

Family by family within the clan. The family of Zimri was taken.

Man by man within the family. Achan was taken.

Can you imagine being Achan in those moments? Watching the circle narrow? Knowing what was buried under your tent? Knowing that with each step, the truth was getting closer?

Joshua confronted him: "My son, give glory to the LORD, the God of Israel, and honor him. Tell me what you have done; do not hide it from me."

And finally, Achan confessed: "It is true! I have sinned against the LORD, the God of Israel." He described the robe, the silver, the gold. He told them where to find it.

Messengers ran to his tent and dug. There it all was, just as he said. They brought the stolen items and spread them out before the LORD and all Israel. The hidden thing was hidden no more.

THE VALLEY OF TROUBLE

What happened next is difficult to read. Achan was taken to a valley, along with his sons and daughters, his cattle, his donkeys, his sheep, his tent, and everything he owned. All of Israel was there.

Joshua said, "Why have you brought this trouble on us? The LORD will bring trouble on you today."

Then all Israel stoned him. They burned everything. They piled rocks over him.

The place was named the Valley of Achor—the Valley of Trouble—because of the trouble Achan had caused.

This is brutal. There's no way around it. The punishment seems extreme to us—not just Achan, but his whole family destroyed.

Why so severe? Because this was the first major act of disobedience after entering the Promised Land. God was establishing a principle that would echo through Israel's history: sin in the community cannot be tolerated. Hidden disobedience affects everyone. The covenant demands faithfulness.

There's also something deeper going on. Achan had taken things that were "devoted" to God—things that belonged exclusively to the Lord. By taking them, Achan had aligned himself with the devoted things. He had made himself like Jericho, like the Canaanites who were marked for destruction. A man from the tribe of Judah had effectively become a Canaanite by his actions.

The contrast with Rahab is striking. Rahab was a Canaanite who believed in Israel's God and joined Israel. Achan was an Israelite who acted like a Canaanite and was destroyed. Your heritage doesn't determine your destiny—your faith and obedience do.

THE SECOND CHANCE AT AI

After Achan's sin was dealt with, the text says simply: "Then the LORD turned from his fierce anger." The barrier was removed. God was with Israel again.

Now God spoke to Joshua with words of encouragement: "Do not be afraid; do not be discouraged. Take the whole army with you, and go up and attack Ai. For I have delivered into your hands the king of Ai, his people, his city and his land."

This time, there were no shortcuts. No "just send a couple thousand guys." The whole army went. And this time, God gave specific battle instructions.

The plan was an ambush. Joshua would send a force to hide behind the city. Then he would lead the main army to the front of Ai and pretend to be defeated—just like before. When the men of Ai chased them out, the hidden force would rush in and capture the city.

It worked perfectly.

The king of Ai saw the Israelite army and led his entire force out to attack them. Joshua and the main army retreated, drawing every last defender away from the city. The ambush force entered the unguarded city and set it on fire.

When the men of Ai looked back and saw smoke rising from their city, they realized they were trapped. The Israelite army that had been fleeing suddenly turned around. The ambush force came out of the burning city. The men of Ai were caught in the middle with nowhere to go. Not one of them survived.

The victory was complete. What had been an embarrassing defeat became a decisive triumph. This time, God had given them permission to keep the livestock and plunder for themselves—a different rule than at Jericho, showing that God's commands aren't always identical but always matter.

THE ALTAR ON MOUNT EBAL

After the victory, Joshua did something that might seem surprising. Before moving on to the next battle, he led the people on a journey to Mount Ebal—about twenty miles north.

There, in obedience to instructions Moses had given years earlier, Joshua built an altar of uncut stones. The people offered burnt offerings and fellowship offerings. Joshua wrote a copy of the Law of Moses on stones.

Then the entire nation gathered—half on Mount Ebal and half on Mount Gerizim, with the valley between them. Joshua read the entire Law out loud, including all the blessings that would come from obedience and all the curses that would come from disobedience. Every man, woman, child, and foreigner heard the words.

Why do this now? Why pause the military campaign for a religious ceremony? Because Israel needed to remember what really mattered. Victory over Ai was meaningless if they forgot why they were there. The land wasn't just real estate to conquer—it was the place where God's people would live under God's covenant. Military success without spiritual faithfulness would lead nowhere good.

The ceremony at Mount Ebal was a reset. After the disaster of Achan and the second victory at Ai, Israel needed to recommit themselves to the covenant. They needed to hear again what God required. They needed to be reminded that blessings come from obedience and curses come from rebellion.

The whole journey—from Jericho's triumph to Ai's defeat to Ai's victory to Ebal's renewal—was really about one thing: would Israel trust and obey God, or would they go their own way?

WHAT THIS MEANS FOR US

So what does this story about a man who stole some treasure three thousand years ago have to do with your life?

First, hidden sin affects more than just you. Achan thought his secret was private. But his disobedience led to thirty-six soldiers dead and an entire nation humiliated. Our sin is never as contained as we think. What we do in secret ripples outward in ways we can't predict.

Second, you can't hide from God. Achan buried his treasure where no one could see it. But God knew exactly what was under that tent. There is nothing hidden that will not be revealed. Living with integrity means living as though God sees everything—because he does.

Third, overconfidence leads to disaster. Israel attacked Ai without seeking God, assuming victory was automatic. They had stopped depending on him. Success can make us careless. The moment we think we've got this figured out on our own is the moment we're most vulnerable.

Fourth, confession matters. When Achan was confronted, he finally told the truth. His confession didn't save him from the consequences, but it gave glory to God by acknowledging the truth. When we sin, the path forward begins with honest confession—to God and often to others.

Fifth, God gives second chances to communities. Israel failed at Ai, but God didn't abandon them. After the sin was dealt with, he gave them another opportunity. The same city that had defeated them became their victory. Our failures don't have to define our future.

TALKING POINTS

Here are some things to think about and discuss:

1. **Achan saw, coveted, and took.** Why do you think temptation often follows this pattern? How can recognizing the pattern help us resist?
2. **One man's secret sin led to Israel's shocking defeat at Ai.** Why do you think God held all of Israel responsible for Achan's sin? What does this teach us about how our actions affect our communities—our families, churches, teams?
3. **Joshua was ready to give up after the defeat at Ai.** Have you ever felt like giving up after a failure? What brought you back?
4. **The second attack on Ai worked because Israel followed God's specific plan.** What's the difference between acting on our own ideas and acting on God's direction?
5. **After the victory, Joshua led the people in a ceremony of covenant renewal.** Why is it important to pause after both failures and successes to remember our commitment to God?

The Valley of Trouble lay behind them. The altar on Mount Ebal stood as a witness. Israel had learned—painfully—that hidden sin brings disaster and that renewed obedience opens the door to blessing.

But they weren't alone in the land. Other cities had heard about Jericho. Other kings were watching. And they were starting to make plans of their own.

Turn the page.

5

THE TRICK AND THE LONGEST DAY

In *Shrek Forever After*, Shrek makes a terrible mistake. He's feeling overwhelmed by his life—the responsibilities, the routines, the constant demands. He misses the old days when he was a feared ogre with no obligations. So when a strange little man named Rumpelstiltskin offers him a deal—one day as a "real ogre" in exchange for one day from his past—Shrek signs the contract without reading the fine print.

Big mistake.

Rumpelstiltskin took the day Shrek was born. And suddenly Shrek is trapped in an alternate reality where he never existed, Far Far Away is a nightmare kingdom, and everything he loves is gone. He made a deal without understanding what he was agreeing to, and now he's stuck with the consequences.

Joshua 9 tells a similar story. A group of clever neighbors pretended to be something they weren't, and Israel made a deal without asking God for guidance. By the time they realized they'd been fooled, it was too late. They had sworn an oath, and breaking it wasn't an option.

But here's where the story gets interesting: God turned the whole mess into something nobody expected. And along the way, he gave Israel the most extraordinary day in military history—a day when the sun itself seemed to stand still.

THE COALITION FORMS

After the victories at Jericho and Ai, and the covenant renewal at Mount Ebal, word was spreading fast throughout Canaan. Every king in the land had heard what Israel's God had done.

The response was massive. Kings from the hill country, the western foothills, and all along the Mediterranean coast formed an alliance. Six different people groups—Hittites, Amorites, Canaanites, Perizzites, Hivites, and Jebusites—put aside their differences and prepared to fight together against Israel.

This was serious. Instead of facing one city at a time, Israel now faced a united front of multiple kingdoms. The opposition was getting organized. But not everyone in Canaan chose to fight.

THE VISITORS FROM "FAR AWAY"

The people of Gibeon had heard the same news as everyone else. They knew about the Jordan River drying up. They knew about Jericho's walls falling flat. They knew about Ai's destruction. And they knew something else too—they knew what God had commanded Israel to do.

Somehow, the Gibeonites had learned that Israel was supposed to completely destroy the peoples living in Canaan, but they were allowed to make peace with cities that were "very far away." Cities close by had to be wiped out. Cities at a distance could surrender and become servants.

So the Gibeonites came up with a plan. They loaded their donkeys with worn-out sacks and cracked, mended wineskins. They put on patched sandals and ragged clothes. They packed bread that was dry and crumbly. Everything about them screamed "long journey."

Then they traveled to Israel's camp at Gilgal and said, "We have come from a distant country. Make a treaty with us."

The Israelites were suspicious. "Maybe you actually live nearby," they said. "How can we make a treaty with you?"

The Gibeonites doubled down on their act. "We are your servants," they said. "We've come because of the fame of the LORD your God. We heard about everything he did in Egypt and to the kings east of the Jordan. Our elders sent us with provisions for the journey. Look at this bread—it was warm when we packed it, and now it's dry and moldy. These wineskins were new; now they're cracked. Our clothes and sandals are worn out from the very long journey."

It was convincing. The evidence seemed solid. The story made sense. And then Israel made their fatal mistake.

THE MISSING QUESTION

The text puts it bluntly: "The Israelites sampled their provisions but did not inquire of the LORD." They looked at the evidence. They examined the moldy bread and cracked wineskins. They used their own judgment and reasoning. And based on what they could see with their eyes, they concluded the Gibeonites were telling the truth. But they never asked God.

God had given Israel a way to seek his guidance when they weren't sure what to do. Through the high priest, they could inquire of the Lord and get direction. But this time, they skipped that step. They trusted their own observations instead.

Joshua made a treaty of peace with the Gibeonites. The leaders of Israel swore an oath to let them live. Three days later, Israel discovered the truth.

THE TERRIBLE DISCOVERY

The Gibeonites weren't from a distant country. They lived just twenty miles away. Their cities were right in the middle of the territory Israel was supposed to conquer.

Israel had been completely fooled.

The Israelites set out and reached the Gibeonite cities on the third day. They found thriving towns full of people who should have been destroyed according to God's commands. And now Israel was bound by an oath not to harm them.

The whole congregation grumbled against the leaders. "You made a deal with them? These people? The ones we're supposed to drive out?"

But the leaders stood firm. "We have sworn to them by the LORD, the God of Israel. We cannot touch them now. If we break our oath, God's wrath will fall on us."

This is crucial: even though the oath was obtained through deception, Israel still had to keep it. An oath sworn in God's name couldn't be broken just because you were tricked. God's name was attached to that promise, and breaking it would dishonor him.

Think about what this means. The Gibeonites lied. They manipulated. They deceived Israel completely. And yet Israel was still bound by their word. Because once you swear by

God's name, the oath matters more than how you were tricked into making it.

THE CURSE AND THE BLESSING

Joshua summoned the Gibeonites and confronted them: "Why did you deceive us? You said you lived far away, but you're our neighbors."

The Gibeonites were honest now: "We were clearly told that the LORD your God commanded Moses to give you this whole land and to wipe out all its inhabitants. We were terrified for our lives. We're in your hands now. Do whatever seems right to you."

Joshua pronounced their sentence: "You are now under a curse. You will always serve as woodcutters and water carriers for the house of my God."

The Gibeonites' response? "We are now in your hands. Do to us whatever seems good and right to you."

So Joshua saved them from the Israelites who wanted to kill them, and he made them permanent servants—woodcutters and water carriers for the tabernacle and for the community.

Here's something interesting: this arrangement, which started as a curse, actually put the Gibeonites at the center of Israel's worship. They spent their days at the tabernacle, serving the house of God. They were foreigners who had deceived their way into Israel, and yet they ended up closer to God's presence than many Israelites would ever be.

Centuries later, we find Gibeonites listed among the people who returned from exile to rebuild Jerusalem's walls. They had been fully integrated into God's people. What began as trickery ended with transformation.

THE ALLIANCE ATTACKS

But the story doesn't end there. When the king of Jerusalem—a man named Adoni-Zedek—heard that Gibeon had made peace with Israel, he panicked.

Gibeon wasn't a small village. It was an important city, as big as a royal capital, with a reputation for mighty warriors. If a city that strong chose to surrender rather than fight, what chance did anyone else have?

Even worse, Gibeon's location was strategic. It sat on major roads connecting different parts of Canaan. With Gibeon as an ally, Israel now controlled a huge swath of the central highlands. The king of Jerusalem felt the noose tightening.

So Adoni-Zedek sent urgent messages to four other kings: Hoham of Hebron, Piram of Jarmuth, Japhia of Lachish, and Debir of Eglon. "Come help me attack Gibeon," he said, "because they've made peace with Joshua and the Israelites."

The five kings combined their armies and marched against Gibeon. This wasn't just revenge for Gibeon's "betrayal" of the Canaanite cause—it was also a test. Would Israel actually defend these people they had just made a treaty with? If Israel abandoned Gibeon, maybe their promises meant nothing after all.

The Gibeonites sent an urgent message to Joshua at Gilgal: "Don't abandon your servants! Come quickly and save us! All these Amorite kings have joined forces against us!"

And now the treaty that began with deception became a test of Israel's integrity.

GOD SPEAKS

Before Joshua moved, God spoke to him directly: "Do not be

afraid of them. I have given them into your hand. Not one of them will be able to stand against you."

This is so important. After the mess with the Gibeonites—after Israel had failed to ask God's guidance and gotten themselves tricked into an oath—God didn't abandon them. He didn't say, "You made this bed, now lie in it." Instead, he gave Joshua encouragement and promise.

God was going to use this situation. The treaty that seemed like a mistake would become the occasion for one of the greatest victories in Israel's history.

Joshua marched all night from Gilgal to Gibeon—about twenty miles uphill. He arrived and launched a surprise attack at dawn. The five kings and their armies were caught completely off guard.

THE BATTLE OF GIBEON

What happened next was extraordinary. The Lord threw the enemy into confusion before Israel. The Israelites struck them with a great blow at Gibeon, then chased them along the road that went up to Beth Horon, cutting them down all the way to Azekah and Makkedah.

But Israel's swords weren't the deadliest weapons that day. As the enemy fled down the road from Beth Horon, the Lord hurled large hailstones from the sky. Massive chunks of ice rained down on the fleeing armies. The text says more died from the hailstones than from Israelite swords.

This was God fighting for his people. The Creator of the universe was using his creation—the weather itself—as a weapon against the enemies of Israel.

THE DAY THE SUN STOOD STILL

Then came the most famous part of the story. On that day, Joshua spoke to the Lord in the presence of all Israel. He said: "Sun, stand still over Gibeon, and moon, over the Valley of Aijalon." And the sun stood still, and the moon stopped, until the nation took vengeance on its enemies. The text tells us: "There has never been a day like it before or since, when the LORD listened to a human being. Surely the LORD was fighting for Israel!"

What exactly happened? People have debated this for centuries. Some believe the earth literally stopped rotating. Others think God prolonged the darkness of a storm, giving Israel cover for their attack. Still others suggest God bent light in miraculous ways to give the appearance of extended daylight—or extended darkness.

Here's what we know for certain: something unprecedented happened. The day was unique in all of human history. God responded to Joshua's prayer in a way he had never done before and has never done since. The Creator intervened in his creation to give his people victory.

The "how" is mysterious. The "why" is clear: God was fighting for Israel.

The five kings themselves fled and hid in a cave at Makkedah. Joshua had the cave sealed with large stones, posted guards, and told the army to keep pursuing the enemy. When the battle was over, Joshua brought out the five kings, had his commanders put their feet on the kings' necks as a symbol of complete victory, and then executed them.

The southern campaign had begun with a bang—or rather, with hailstones and a miracle in the sky.

WHAT THIS MEANS FOR US

So what do we take from this wild story of trickery, treaties, and cosmic intervention?

First, don't skip the step of asking God. Israel's whole problem with the Gibeonites started because they didn't inquire of the Lord. They trusted their own eyes, their own reasoning, their own judgment. The moldy bread seemed convincing. But what seems obvious to us isn't always true, and what seems reasonable isn't always God's will. Before making big decisions, ask.

Second, keep your word even when it costs you. Israel was tricked into their oath, but they kept it anyway because God's name was attached to it. Integrity means honoring your commitments even when it's inconvenient, even when you were deceived, even when you'd rather not. Your word should mean something.

Third, God can redeem our mistakes. Israel never should have made that treaty without asking God. But once they did, God worked with the situation. He turned the defense of Gibeon into the conquest of five enemy kingdoms. He took Israel's failure and wove it into his plan. That doesn't mean we should be careless—but it does mean our mistakes aren't the end of the story.

Fourth, God fights for his people. Hailstones from heaven. The sun responding to a man's prayer. The Creator wielding his creation as a weapon. When God is on your side, the forces of nature themselves become your allies. This doesn't mean life will be easy or that we'll never face opposition. But it means the ultimate outcome is never in doubt.

Fifth, unexpected people end up in unexpected places. The Gibeonites started as deceivers trying to save their own skins. They ended up as servants at God's tabernacle, integrated into his people, listed among the faithful who rebuilt Jerusalem. Sometimes the most unlikely people find their way to the center of God's story.

TALKING POINTS

Here are some things to think about and discuss:

1. **The Gibeonites went to elaborate lengths to deceive Israel.** Have you ever been fooled by something that seemed totally convincing? What made it believable?
2. **Israel didn't ask God before making the treaty.** Why do you think they skipped that step? When are you most tempted to make decisions without praying first?
3. **Even though Israel was tricked, they still kept their oath.** Why was this so important? What does it teach us about integrity?
4. **The Gibeonites ended up serving at the tabernacle—what started as a curse became a connection to God.** Have you ever seen something that seemed bad turn into something good?
5. **God fought for Israel with hailstones and a miracle in the sky.** What does this tell us about God's power over creation? About his commitment to his people?

The five kings were defeated. The southern campaign was underway. God had shown himself to be the cosmic warrior who could command the weather and even the sun itself. But the northern kings had heard the news too. And they were gathering their own alliance—bigger than anything Israel had faced yet.

Turn the page.

6

THE FINAL BOSS

In almost every video game, there's a pattern you learn to expect. You fight your way through level after level. The enemies get harder. The challenges get tougher. You face mini-bosses along the way—powerful opponents that test everything you've learned so far. And then, when you've proven yourself through all of that, you face the final boss.

The final boss is always the biggest threat. The most powerful enemy. The one with the most resources, the strongest weapons, and the largest army. It's the opponent the whole game has been building toward.

In *The Legend of Zelda: Breath of the Wild*, it's Calamity Ganon. In the *Avengers* movies, it's Thanos. In *Star Wars*, it's the Emperor. The final boss represents everything that stands against the hero, gathered into one ultimate confrontation.

For Joshua and Israel, the final boss was Jabin, king of Hazor. Everything in the conquest of Canaan had been building to this moment. Israel had crossed the Jordan. They had taken Jericho and Ai. They had survived the Gibeonite deception and turned it into victory. They had crushed the southern coalition of five kings in a battle where hailstones fell from heaven and the sun itself responded to Joshua's prayer.

But the north remained unconquered. And in the north, Hazor was waiting—the largest, most powerful city in all of Canaan, ready to bring together the biggest army Israel had ever faced.

THE NORTHERN ALLIANCE

When Jabin, king of Hazor, heard what Joshua had done to the southern coalition, he didn't panic. He didn't hide behind his walls and hope Israel would pass him by. Instead, he did exactly what Adoni-Zedek had done in the south—he sent messages to every king he could reach.

But Jabin's alliance was even bigger. The text lists king after king, region after region, people group after people group. The Canaanites from the east and west. The Amorites, Hittites, Perizzites, and Jebusites from the hill country. The Hivites from below Mount Hermon. Kings from Madon, Shimron, and Acshaph joined forces with Hazor.

When all these armies gathered together at the Waters of Merom—a location in the northern highlands—the text says they were "as numerous as the sand on the seashore."

And they brought something the southern coalition hadn't: horses and chariots.

This matters because horses and chariots were the ancient equivalent of tanks. They were the most advanced military technology of the age. On flat ground, a chariot force could devastate infantry. The Canaanites of the northern valleys had built their entire military strategy around these powerful weapons.

Israel had none. They were still just foot soldiers—former slaves who had grown up in the wilderness, armed with whatever weapons they could carry. Now they faced a professional military force with cavalry and war machines, gathered from every corner of northern Canaan.

If this were a video game, this would be the level where the difficulty spike makes you wonder if victory is even possible.

GOD SPEAKS AGAIN

Before the battle, the LORD spoke to Joshua: "Do not be afraid of them. By this time tomorrow I will hand all of them over to Israel, slain. You are to hamstring their horses and burn their chariots."

Two things stand out in this promise. First, the timing: "by this time tomorrow." God wasn't just promising victory eventually—he was promising it within twenty-four hours. The largest army Israel had ever faced would be completely defeated by the next day.

Second, the instructions about the horses and chariots. God didn't tell Joshua to capture the chariots and use them for Israel's army. He told him to destroy them. Hamstring the horses (cut the tendons in their legs so they couldn't run) and burn the chariots.

Why? Because God didn't want Israel relying on military technology. He wanted them relying on him. If Israel had the best chariots in Canaan, they might start thinking their victories came from superior weapons. But without chariots, every victory would clearly be God's doing.

This is a principle that runs throughout the Bible: God often keeps his people in positions where they have to depend on him rather than on their own resources.

THE SURPRISE ATTACK

Joshua didn't wait for the enemy to come to him. He marched his army to the Waters of Merom and launched a surprise attack.

The text describes what happened in rapid-fire succession: "The LORD gave them into the hand of Israel. They defeated them and pursued them all the way to Greater Sidon, to Misrephoth Maim, and to the Valley of Mizpah on the east, until no survivors were left."

Look at those place names on a map, and you'll see something remarkable. Greater Sidon is on the Mediterranean coast, far to the northwest. Misrephoth Maim is in the northeast. The Valley of Mizpah is to the east. The pursuit went in multiple directions, covering an enormous geographical area.

This wasn't just a battle—it was a rout. The greatest army Canaan had ever assembled scattered in every direction, and Israel chased them down until none were left.

And Joshua did exactly what God commanded: he hamstrung the horses and burned the chariots.

HAZOR BURNS

After the battle, Joshua turned back and attacked Hazor itself. Hazor was no ordinary city. The text calls it "the head of all these kingdoms"—the capital, the center, the most important city in all of northern Canaan. Archaeological excavations have confirmed this. Hazor was massive, covering over two hundred acres, with impressive fortifications and international connections. Documents from across the ancient Near East mention Hazor as a major power.

Joshua captured Hazor, killed its king, and put everyone in the city to the sword. Then he did something he had done to only two other cities in the entire conquest: he burned it to the ground.

Throughout the campaign, Israel had not burned the cities they conquered. God had promised them "large, flourishing cities you did not build, houses filled with all kinds of good things you did not provide." The plan was to move into these cities, not destroy them.

But three cities received special treatment: Jericho, Ai, and Hazor. These three were burned. Jericho was the first city, the gateway to the land. Ai was where Israel had learned the hard lesson about sin in the camp. And Hazor was the final boss, the greatest center of resistance to God's purposes. All three were reduced to ashes.

WHAT THE CONQUEST REALLY LOOKED LIKE

After describing the defeat of the northern coalition, the text pauses to give us some important perspective. "Joshua waged war against all these kings for a long time."

Wait—a long time? The way the story has been told, it might seem like the conquest happened quickly. One battle after another, victory upon victory, enemies falling like dominoes.

But that's not what actually happened. The best estimate is that the conquest took about seven years. Seven years of marching, fighting, camping, regrouping, and fighting again. Seven years of trusting God through battle after battle, city after city.

The Bible often compresses time in its storytelling, focusing on the key events and skipping over the long stretches in between. What looks like a few pages of reading was actually years of living.

This matters because it reminds us that God's work often takes longer than we expect. The Israelites didn't conquer Canaan in a weekend. They did it day by day, month by month, year by year, trusting God through the long haul.

WHY THE CANAANITES FOUGHT

The text also explains something important about why things happened the way they did: "Except for the Hivites living in Gibeon, not one city made a treaty of peace with the Israelites, who took them all in battle. For it was the LORD himself who hardened their hearts to wage war against Israel, so that he might destroy them totally, exterminating them without mercy, as the LORD had commanded Moses."

This is striking. The Gibeonites had found a way to make peace, even if it was through deception. Rahab had found a way to be saved through faith. But everyone else chose to fight.

Why? The text says God hardened their hearts.

This is the same language used about Pharaoh in Egypt. When God sent Moses to demand Israel's freedom, Pharaoh refused again and again, and the text says God hardened Pharaoh's heart. But if you read the Exodus story carefully, you'll see that Pharaoh hardened his own heart first. His stubbornness came from within, and God confirmed him in the path he had already chosen.

The same seems to be true of the Canaanites. They had heard about Israel's God. They had witnessed the miracles.

They had every opportunity to respond like Rahab did—with fear that led to faith. Instead, they chose defiance. And God let them have what they chose.

There's something sobering here. God's patience is real, but it's not unlimited. There comes a point when people who keep refusing God get confirmed in their refusal. The Canaanites had centuries to turn from their wickedness. Instead, their sins kept growing worse until the time for judgment finally came.

THE GIANTS FALL

One more military campaign gets mentioned: the defeat of the Anakites. Remember way back in the book of Numbers, when Moses sent twelve spies into Canaan? Ten of them came back terrified, saying, "We saw the descendants of Anak there. We seemed like grasshoppers in our own eyes, and we looked the same to them."

The Anakites were giants—or at least, they were remembered as giants. They were the people who had frightened Israel so badly that the whole nation refused to enter the land forty years earlier. That generation died in the wilderness because they looked at the Anakites and forgot about their God.

Now, finally, Joshua led an army against these legendary warriors. He cut them down from Hebron, from Debir, from Anab, and from all the hill country. By the time he was finished, no Anakites remained in Israelite territory. A few survived in Gaza, Gath, and Ashdod—Philistine cities on the coast—but they were no longer a threat to God's people.

The giants that had terrified their parents were now defeated by their children.

What made the difference? Not superior numbers or better weapons. The difference was that this generation trusted God instead of trembling at the size of their enemies.

THE LAND HAS REST

And then comes one of the most beautiful sentences in the whole book: "So Joshua took the entire land, just as the LORD had directed Moses, and he gave it as an inheritance to Israel according to their tribal divisions. Then the land had rest from war."

Rest.

After forty years of wandering in the wilderness. After seven years of conquest. After battle upon battle, city after city, enemy after enemy—finally, rest.

The Hebrew word for "rest" here connects to something bigger. Way back in Deuteronomy, God had promised that when Israel entered the land and defeated their enemies, they would find rest. It was part of the covenant blessing. The wandering would end. The fighting would cease. God's people would live in peace in the land God had given them.

Joshua 11 records the fulfillment of that promise. The major battles were over. The land was subdued. The inheritance could now be distributed.

This doesn't mean every square inch of Canaan was conquered—later chapters make clear that plenty of territory still needed to be taken. But the decisive victories had been won. The major powers had been broken. The rest was a matter of settlement and consolidation.

THE SCOREBOARD: THIRTY-ONE KINGS

Chapter 12 functions like a scoreboard at the end of a championship game. It's a list—a detailed, comprehensive list—of every king Israel defeated.

First, it recounts the victories under Moses, east of the Jordan River: King Sihon of the Amorites and King Og of Bashan. These battles happened before Joshua even took command, but they're included because they were part of the same story. The same God who gave victory to Moses gave victory to Joshua.

Then comes the main list: thirty-one kings defeated west of the Jordan under Joshua's leadership.

The king of Jericho—one.

The king of Ai—one.

The king of Jerusalem—one.

The king of Hebron—one.

On and on the list goes, city after city, king after king. Some of these names we recognize from the stories we've read: Lachish, Eglon, Gezer, Hazor. Others are cities we haven't heard about, places whose conquests weren't described in detail but were just as real.

Thirty-one kings. Thirty-one defeated enemies. Thirty-one testimonies to the faithfulness of God.

The list might seem tedious to read, but it serves an important purpose. It's proof. It's evidence. It's the documentation that everything God promised actually happened.

When God told Abraham that his descendants would inherit this land, it was just a promise. When God told Moses to lead Israel out of Egypt toward a land flowing with milk and honey, it was still future. When God told Joshua that everywhere his foot stepped would be given to him, it required faith to believe.

But now? Now there was a list. Thirty-one conquered kings. Thirty-one fulfilled promises. Thirty-one reasons to trust that the God who made promises is the God who keeps them.

WHAT THIS MEANS FOR US

So what do we take from this final campaign and victory tally?

First, God's enemies ultimately cannot stand against him. Jabin gathered the largest army Canaan had ever seen—horses, chariots, soldiers as numerous as sand on the seashore. It didn't matter. By the next day, they were destroyed. No amount of human power can ultimately resist God's purposes.

Second, God doesn't want us trusting in human resources. Burn the chariots. Hamstring the horses. Don't build your confidence on technology, weapons, wealth, or anything else that can substitute for dependence on God. He is the source of victory, and he wants us to know it.

Third, faithful obedience is often a long journey. Seven years of conquest. Thousands of days of trusting God and following his commands. The Christian life isn't usually one dramatic moment—it's years of walking with God, day after day, battle after battle.

Fourth, there comes a time when resistance to God hardens into judgment. The Canaanites had opportunities. They had Rahab's example. They had the Gibeonites' example. They chose to fight anyway, and God let them have the consequences of their choice.

Fifth, the giants that terrify one generation can be de-

feated by the next. The Anakites paralyzed Israel's parents with fear. Israel's children cut them down. What changed wasn't the size of the giants—it was the faith of the people facing them.

TALKING POINTS

Here are some things to think about and discuss:

1. **When Israel faced a massive coalition, God commanded them to hamstring the horses and burn the chariots after the victory.** Why do you think God told Joshua to do this instead of keeping them for Israel's army? What does this teach us about trusting in resources versus trusting in God?
2. **The conquest took about seven years.** Does that surprise you? What does it teach us about how God often works—quickly or slowly?
3. **The Canaanites had the same information Rahab had, but they responded differently.** What made the difference? What does this teach us about how people respond to God?
4. **The Anakites terrified one generation but were defeated by the next.** What "giants" in your life seem overwhelming? How does faith change how we face them?
5. **Chapter 12 lists thirty-one defeated kings.** Why do you think the Bible includes lists like this? What purpose do they serve?

The battles were over. The scoreboard was complete. Thirty-one kings had fallen, from the southern desert to the northern mountains.

But conquering the land was only half the story. Now came the task of dividing it up—deciding which tribe would live where, which family would inherit what, and how God's people would actually settle into the home he had given them.

The war was ending. A new chapter was about to begin.

Turn the page.

7

EVERYBODY GETS A PIECE

Imagine this: your family just won the biggest lottery jackpot in history. We're talking billions of dollars. The lawyers are called. The accountants are ready. And now comes the moment everyone has been waiting for—deciding who gets what.

Every family member gathers around a huge table. There are bank accounts to divide, properties to distribute, and investments to allocate. Some people get houses in the mountains. Others get beachfront condos. Someone inherits the family business. Someone else gets the vacation home.

Now imagine this process taking weeks. Maybe months. Every single asset needs to be documented. Every property needs clear boundaries. Every inheritance needs to be official, legal, and written down so there's no confusion later.

Sounds intense, right? Maybe even a little boring compared to action movies?

But here's the thing: for the family members sitting around that table, this is the most important moment of their lives. Everything they've waited for, everything they've hoped for, everything that was promised to them—it all becomes real right here.

That's what Joshua 13–21 is about. The battles were over. The conquest was complete. Thirty-one kings had been defeated. And now came the moment Israel had been waiting for since Abraham first heard God's promise nearly five hundred years earlier: It was time to divide the land.

THE LONGEST LIST YOU'LL EVER SKIM

Let's be honest about something. If you flip through Joshua 13–21 in your Bible, you'll find page after page of names, boundaries, and cities. It looks like this: "The boundary went up to Beth Hoglah and passed north of Beth Arabah to the Stone of Bohan son of Reuben. The boundary then went up to Debir from the Valley of Achor and turned north to Gilgal..." And on and on it goes. Borders that twist and turn. Lists of cities with names you can't pronounce. Details about who lives where and which tribe gets what.

Why would the Bible include all this? Because to the people who received this land, every single detail mattered.

Think about it this way: if you had been wandering in the wilderness for forty years, sleeping in tents, never owning anything, never having a permanent home—and then someone finally said, "Here's your land, forever"—wouldn't you want every boundary line written down? Wouldn't you want to know exactly which cities belonged to your family?

These chapters aren't just ancient real estate documents. They're proof that God keeps his promises.

THE SETUP

Before the land could be divided, Joshua got some important instructions from God. "You are old and advanced in years," God said, "and there remains yet very much land to be possessed."

Interesting. Even though the major battles were won and the land was conquered, there were still pockets of territory that needed to be taken. The overall victory was complete, but the details weren't finished.

God told Joshua that he would drive out the remaining inhabitants himself. Joshua's job now wasn't to fight—it was to divide.

The division would happen in two stages. First, the territories east of the Jordan River (which Moses had already assigned to Reuben, Gad, and half of Manasseh). Then, the territories west of the Jordan for the remaining nine and a half tribes.

And here's something important: the land wasn't divided by human preference or political power. It was divided by lot—essentially a sacred random drawing that God controlled. Nobody could claim they got cheated. Nobody could accuse the leaders of favoritism. God himself determined who got what.

CALEB STEPS FORWARD

Before the main distribution began, an old man pushed his way to the front of the crowd. His name was Caleb. He was eighty-five years old. And he had been waiting for this moment for forty-five years.

Remember way back when Moses sent twelve spies into Canaan? Ten came back terrified, but two—Joshua and Caleb—trusted God and said Israel could take the land. Because the people listened to the fearful spies instead, that entire generation was sentenced to die in the wilderness.

But God made a promise to Caleb: "The land on which your feet have walked will be your inheritance, because you have wholly followed the LORD."

Now, forty-five years later, Caleb was collecting on that promise. "I was forty years old when Moses sent me to spy out the land," Caleb told Joshua. "I brought back an honest report. My brothers made the people's hearts melt with fear, but I wholly followed the LORD my God."

And then this eighty-five-year-old warrior made an audacious request: "Give me this hill country that the LORD promised me that day. You heard then that the Anakites were there, with large fortified cities. Perhaps the LORD will be with me, and I shall drive them out."

The Anakites! The giants! The very people who had terrified the spies forty-five years earlier. Caleb wasn't asking for easy territory. He wanted the land that still had giants in it.

Joshua blessed Caleb and gave him Hebron. And Caleb drove out the three sons of Anak from there. At eighty-five years old. That's what wholehearted devotion looks like over the long haul.

THE BIG TRIBES GET THEIR SHARE

After Caleb's inspiring claim, the main distribution began. Judah went first because Judah was the most important tribe. Jacob had blessed Judah centuries earlier with a prophecy about kings coming from his line. (Spoiler: King David would come from Judah. So would Jesus.) Judah's territory was massive—the entire southern portion of Canaan, from the wilderness to the Mediterranean Sea.

The tribe of Joseph came next—actually, Joseph's two sons, Ephraim and Manasseh. Remember how Jacob adopted Joseph's sons and gave them equal status with his own sons? That meant Joseph effectively got a double portion. Ephraim and Manasseh together received a huge chunk of the central highlands.

But here's where things got interesting. The Joseph tribes complained to Joshua: "The hill country isn't enough for us. There are too many of us!"

Joshua's response was basically: "If you're so numerous and powerful, go clear the forests and expand your territory. Drive out the Canaanites yourselves."

The Joseph tribes protested: "But the Canaanites have iron chariots!"

Joshua didn't budge. "You are numerous and powerful. You will drive them out."

Not everyone who received an inheritance received it gracefully. Some people wanted more without working for it. Joshua expected the tribes to trust God and act.

FIVE SISTERS WHO CHANGED THE LAW

Here's a story that's easy to miss in all the boundary lists, but it's remarkable. A man named Zelophehad had died without any sons. He had five daughters: Mahlah, Noah, Hoglah, Milcah, and Tirzah. In that culture, land normally passed through sons. Daughters didn't inherit. So when Zelophehad died, his family's inheritance was in jeopardy.

But these five sisters didn't accept that. Years earlier, when Moses was still alive, they had approached him with their case:

"Why should our father's name disappear from his clan just because he had no son? Give us property among our father's relatives."

Moses took their case to God. And God's answer was clear: "What Zelophehad's daughters are saying is right. You must certainly give them property as an inheritance among their father's relatives." God changed the inheritance law because five women had the courage to speak up.

Now, in Joshua's day, those same five sisters came forward to claim what God had promised. They went to Eleazar the priest, to Joshua, and to the leaders, and reminded them of what the Lord had commanded Moses.

Joshua gave them their inheritance among their father's brothers. Five portions for five faithful women who trusted God and weren't afraid to ask.

THE TRIBE WITHOUT LAND

One tribe didn't appear in the land distribution: Levi. The Levites—the priests and their helpers—received no territorial inheritance. Instead, God himself was their inheritance. They would receive portions of the sacrifices the people brought to God. They would live off the tithes and offerings.

But they did need places to live. So instead of territory, the Levites received forty-eight cities scattered throughout all the other tribes' lands. Every tribe contributed cities for the Levites.

This arrangement served multiple purposes. First, it provided for God's ministers. Second, it distributed spiritual leadership throughout the nation—wherever you lived in Israel, there were Levites nearby who could teach the law and lead worship. Third, it prevented any one group from having a monopoly on religious authority.

The Levites were like salt scattered throughout the whole nation, preserving and flavoring everything they touched.

CITIES OF REFUGE

Among the Levitical cities, six had a special purpose: they were cities of refuge. Here's the situation these cities addressed: What happens if someone accidentally kills another person? Not murder—a genuine accident. Maybe an axe head flew off while chopping wood and struck someone. In that culture, the victim's family had the right to pursue justice through a "blood avenger"—a relative who could execute the killer.

But what about accidents? Should someone die for an unintentional killing?

God provided a solution. Six cities—three on each side of the Jordan—were designated as safe havens. Anyone who accidentally killed someone could flee to one of these cities. There, they would be protected from the blood avenger until a proper trial could determine whether the killing was intentional or accidental.

If the killing was ruled accidental, the person could stay in the city of refuge, safe and protected. They had to remain there until the high priest died, at which point they were free to return home.

This system showed God's concern for justice. It protected the innocent from revenge while still taking death seriously. Even accidental killing had consequences—the person had to leave their home and live in exile. But it wasn't execution.

The six cities of refuge were Kedesh, Shechem, and Hebron on the west side of the Jordan, and Bezer, Ramoth, and Golan on the east side. No matter where you were in Israel, one of these cities was within a day's journey.

THE SEVEN SLOW TRIBES

After Judah and Joseph received their territories, seven tribes still hadn't received their inheritance. And apparently, they weren't in any hurry to claim it.

Joshua confronted them: "How long will you wait before you take possession of the land the LORD, the God of your fathers, has given you?"

This is remarkable. God had promised them land. God had fought for them. The territory was theirs for the taking. And they were just … sitting there.

Joshua sent surveyors from each tribe to map out the remaining territory. They divided it into seven portions and brought the descriptions back to Joshua, who cast lots for them at Shiloh.

Sometimes God's people need a push to claim what's already theirs.

THE MOMENT OF COMPLETION

Finally, after all the tribes had received their portions—after Judah and Benjamin and Simeon and Zebulun and Issachar and Asher and Naphtali and Dan—after the cities of refuge were designated and the Levitical cities distributed—after every boundary was marked and every list recorded—Joshua himself received his inheritance. The people gave him

Timnath-serah in the hill country of Ephraim. He rebuilt the city and settled there.

And then comes one of the most powerful conclusions in all of Scripture: "So the LORD gave to Israel all the land that he swore to give to their fathers. And they took possession of it, and they settled there. And the LORD gave them rest on every side just as he had sworn to their fathers. Not one of all their enemies had withstood them, for the LORD had given all their enemies into their hands. Not one word of all the good promises that the LORD had made to the house of Israel had failed; all came to pass."

Read that again slowly.

Not one word failed. Every single promise God made—every one of them—came true.

This is the heart of the book of Joshua. Not the battles. Not the victories. The fulfillment of promises. God said he would give Abraham's descendants this land. It took five hundred years, but he did it. God said he would drive out their enemies. He did it. God said they would find rest. They found it.

Every word came to pass.

WHAT THIS MEANS FOR US

So what do we take from nine chapters of land distribution?

First, God keeps his promises—even when fulfillment takes a long time. Five hundred years from Abraham to Joshua. Forty-five years from Caleb's mission to Caleb's inheritance. God's timing isn't our timing, but his faithfulness is absolute.

Second, inheritance requires action. The land was given by God, but the tribes had to take possession of it. Caleb had to drive out the giants. The Joseph tribes had to clear the forests. The seven slow tribes had to get moving. God gives, but we have to receive.

Third, everyone matters in God's distribution. Every tribe received something. Every clan was recorded. Even five daughters who had no brothers got their rightful inheritance. God's fairness extends to the overlooked and marginalized.

Fourth, God provides for his servants. The Levites had no territory, but they had God himself—and forty-eight cities and portions of every sacrifice. Those who serve God are not forgotten.

Fifth, God cares about justice. The cities of refuge weren't just administrative conveniences—they were God's way of protecting the innocent while still taking life seriously. Justice and mercy met in those six cities.

TALKING POINTS

Here are some things to think about and discuss:

1. **Caleb waited forty-five years to receive what God promised him.** What does his story teach us about patience and faithfulness over the long haul?

2. **The Joseph tribes complained that their territory wasn't enough.** Joshua challenged them to expand it themselves. When do we complain about not having enough instead of working with what God has given us?

3. **Zelophehad's daughters spoke up and changed the inheritance law.** What does their courage teach us about advocating for what's right?

4. **The Levites had no territory—God himself was their**

inheritance. What might it mean for us to consider God as our inheritance rather than material possessions?

5. **The conclusion says "not one word" of God's promises failed.** How does God's track record of faithfulness affect how you trust him with things that haven't happened yet?

The land was divided. The inheritance was secure. Every tribe knew exactly what belonged to them and where their boundaries lay. But the story wasn't quite over. The tribes east of the Jordan were heading home—and they were about to do something that nearly started a civil war.

Turn the page.

8

THE ALMOST WAR AND THE FINAL CHOICE

In the movie *Captain America: Civil War*, the Avengers—heroes who have fought side by side against every kind of enemy—nearly destroy each other. The conflict doesn't start with villains or aliens. It starts with a misunderstanding. One group of heroes believes they're doing the right thing. The other group believes they're protecting what matters most. Both sides have good intentions. Both sides think they're being loyal to what the team stands for.

But because they don't stop to listen—because they assume the worst about each other—friends become enemies. The team that saved the world together comes within inches of tearing itself apart.

Something almost exactly like this happened to Israel right after the conquest was complete. The tribes that had fought together for seven years, that had bled together and trusted God together, came within days of launching a civil war against each other. All because of a misunderstanding about an altar.

GOING HOME

Remember way back at the beginning of the book? Before Israel crossed the Jordan, Joshua had reminded the tribes of Reuben, Gad, and the half-tribe of Manasseh about a promise they had made to Moses. Their families and livestock were already settled on the east side of the Jordan, in land Moses had given them. But the fighting men had promised to cross over and help their brothers conquer the land on the west side.

For seven long years, they had kept that promise. They had left their wives, children, and homes behind. They had fought every battle alongside the other tribes. They had been there at Jericho, at Ai, in the southern and northern campaigns.

Now, finally, the conquest was complete. And Joshua called them together to release them from their service. "You have done all that Moses the servant of the LORD commanded," Joshua told them. "You have obeyed me in everything I commanded. For a long time now—to this very day—you have not deserted your brothers but have carried out the mission the LORD your God gave you." Then he blessed them, loaded them down with plunder—silver, gold, bronze, iron, and clothing—and sent them home.

Mission accomplished. Promise kept. Time to be reunited with their families. It should have been a joyful ending.

THE ALTAR

On their way home, when these eastern tribes reached the Jordan River, they built an altar. Not just any altar. The text describes it as "imposing"—large enough to be seen from a great distance. They built it right there at the boundary between the eastern and western territories, on the west side of the river.

And when the other tribes heard about it, they didn't celebrate. They didn't send congratulations. They gathered for war. The whole assembly of Israel came together at Shiloh, ready to march against their own brothers. The men who had just spent seven years fighting alongside each other were now preparing to fight against each other.

Why such an extreme reaction?

Because God had been very clear: there was only one place where sacrifices were to be offered. The tabernacle. The altar there. Nowhere else. Building an alternative altar meant setting up a rival worship center, which would be rebellion against God himself.

Israel had learned this lesson the hard way. They remembered what happened at Peor, when the nation was seduced into worshipping Moabite gods and a plague killed twenty-four thousand people. They remembered Achan, whose hidden sin brought defeat on the whole nation. They knew that one group's unfaithfulness could bring God's judgment on everyone.

So when they heard about this altar, they assumed the worst. Their brothers had barely crossed the river before abandoning the Lord. Judgment would fall on the whole nation if this wasn't dealt with immediately. Civil war seemed like the only option.

A DELEGATION INSTEAD

But wisdom prevailed. Before launching an attack, the western tribes sent a delegation to investigate. Phinehas, the son of the high priest, led the group, along with ten leaders representing each of the western tribes. These men had the authority to speak for the whole nation. They crossed the Jordan to confront their brothers.

Their speech was direct and uncompromising: "How could you break faith with the God of Israel like this? How could you turn away from the LORD and build yourselves an altar in rebellion against him?" They reminded the eastern tribes of Peor. They reminded them of Achan. They spelled out the consequences: "If you rebel against the LORD today, tomorrow he will be angry with the whole community of Israel."

Then they made an extraordinary offer: "If the land you possess is defiled, come over to the LORD's land, where the LORD's tabernacle stands, and share the land with us."

Think about that. The western tribes were so concerned about maintaining unity with God that they offered to give up portions of their own inheritance rather than see their brothers drift into idolatry.

But they were wrong about the altar. Completely wrong.

THE DEFENSE

The eastern tribes responded with passion—and perhaps a little indignation. "The Mighty One, God, the LORD! The Mighty One, God, the LORD! He knows! And let Israel know!" They called God as their witness with the strongest possible language. Then they explained why they had built the altar.

It wasn't for sacrifices. It wasn't for rebellion. It was the exact opposite. "We did it for fear that some day your descendants might say to ours, 'What do you have to do with the LORD, the God of Israel? The LORD has made the Jordan a boundary between us and you—you Reubenites and Gadites! You have no share in the LORD.'"

They were afraid of being forgotten. The Jordan River was a significant boundary. In future generations, the western tribes might start thinking of the eastern tribes as outsiders. "You don't even live in the real promised land," they might say. "You're not truly part of Israel. You have no right to worship at the tabernacle."

The altar was built as a witness—a permanent reminder that the eastern tribes were fully part of God's people, with every right to worship him at the proper place. "Look at the replica of the LORD's altar," they explained. "Our fathers built it not for burnt offerings and sacrifices, but as a witness between us and you." The altar was never meant to replace the tabernacle. It was meant to point to it.

CRISIS AVERTED

When Phinehas and the delegation heard this explanation, their response was immediate: "Today we know that the LORD is with us, because you have not acted unfaithfully."

They returned to the western tribes with the good news. The assembly that had gathered for war instead praised God. The eastern tribes named their altar "Witness"—a testimony that "the LORD is God."

A civil war was averted. The unity of the nation was preserved. And it happened because both sides cared deeply about the same thing: faithfulness to God and maintaining their relationship with each other.

The story is a powerful reminder that good intentions can

be misread. That assumptions can be wrong. That stopping to ask questions before attacking can save relationships that would otherwise be destroyed.

A LONG TIME LATER

Years passed. Maybe decades. The text tells us that "a long time" after the land had rest, Joshua—now old and near the end of his life—called the leaders of Israel together.

Joshua had been their commander through every battle. He had distributed their inheritance. He had led them faithfully for decades. Now he was about to "go the way of all the earth"—an ancient way of saying he was about to die. He had final words for his people. And like all final words, they mattered.

Joshua's first speech was addressed to the leaders: elders, heads of families, judges, and officials. He reminded them of what God had done—fighting for them, giving them the land, and keeping every single promise. "Not one word has failed of all the good things the LORD your God promised concerning you," Joshua declared. "Every promise has been fulfilled; not one has failed."

But then came a warning. Just as surely as God's promises of blessing had come true, his promises of judgment would also come true if Israel turned away from him. "If you violate the covenant of the LORD your God … and go and serve other gods and bow down to them, the LORD's anger will burn against you, and you will quickly perish from this good land he has given you."

The land belonged to God. He had given it to Israel, but

he could take it away. Their continued presence depended on their continued faithfulness.

THE GATHERING AT SHECHEM

For his final address, Joshua gathered all the tribes at a place heavy with meaning: Shechem. This was where God had first appeared to Abraham and promised to give the land to his descendants. This was where Jacob had purchased a piece of property and built an altar. This was where, earlier in Joshua's leadership, the nation had renewed its covenant at Mount Ebal.

Now, centuries after Abraham first stood here and heard God's promise, Joshua gathered Abraham's descendants—a great nation in possession of the promised land—for one final ceremony.

The speech began with God speaking through Joshua, reviewing the entire history of what he had done for his people:

"I took your father Abraham from the land beyond the Euphrates and led him throughout Canaan."

"I sent Moses and Aaron, and I afflicted the Egyptians … Then I brought you out."

"I brought you to the land of the Amorites … I gave them into your hands."

"I sent the hornet ahead of you … You did not do it with your own sword and bow."

"I gave you a land on which you did not toil and cities you did not build."

Over and over: I did this. I gave that. I fought for you. I provided for you.

The entire history of Israel was a record of God's grace.

THE CHOICE

Then came the challenge that has echoed through the centuries: "Now fear the LORD and serve him with all faithfulness. Throw away the gods your ancestors worshiped beyond the Euphrates River and in Egypt, and serve the LORD."

Wait—gods in Egypt? Gods from beyond the Euphrates? After everything God had done, after all the miracles and victories, some Israelites still had idols in their tents?

Apparently so. The pull of false gods never fully goes away. And Joshua knew it. "But if serving the LORD seems undesirable to you, then choose for yourselves this day whom you will serve, whether the gods your ancestors served beyond the Euphrates, or the gods of the Amorites, in whose land you are living."

Joshua laid out the options clearly. There were no hidden alternatives, no middle ground, no "a little bit of both." It was either the Lord or the false gods. Israel had to choose.

And then Joshua declared his own choice: "But as for me and my household, we will serve the LORD."

The people responded with enthusiasm: "Far be it from us to forsake the LORD to serve other gods! We too will serve the LORD, because he is our God."

THE SOBERING REPLY

Joshua's response to their commitment is startling: "You are not able to serve the LORD." What? They just said they would serve him! Why would Joshua tell them they couldn't? "He is a holy God; he is a jealous God. He will not forgive your rebellion and your sins. If you forsake the LORD and serve foreign gods, he will turn and bring disaster on you."

Joshua wasn't discouraging them from serving God. He was making sure they understood what they were committing to. This wasn't a casual decision. It wasn't a New Year's resolution they could break by February. The God they were pledging themselves to was holy—utterly pure and set apart. He was jealous—refusing to share their devotion with any rival.

Serving this God required everything. Half-hearted commitment wouldn't cut it.

The people insisted: "No! We will serve the LORD."

Joshua accepted their choice: "You are witnesses against yourselves that you have chosen to serve the LORD."

"Yes, we are witnesses."

And so the covenant was renewed. Joshua recorded the words in the Book of the Law of God. He set up a large stone under an oak tree as a permanent witness to what had happened that day. "This stone will be a witness against us," Joshua told them. "It has heard all the words the LORD has said to us." Then he sent the people away, each to their own inheritance.

THREE BURIALS

The book of Joshua ends quietly with three burial notices. Joshua died at 110 years old and was buried in the land of his inheritance. For the first time in the entire book, he is given the same title that had belonged to Moses: "the servant of the LORD." The question raised at the beginning—whether Joshua could be a worthy successor to Moses—was finally answered. He had earned that title through decades of faithful leadership.

Joseph's bones, which the Israelites had carried out of Egypt and through forty years of wilderness wandering, were finally buried at Shechem—the very place where the covenant had just been renewed. A promise made centuries earlier to a dying patriarch was finally kept.

And Eleazar the priest, Aaron's son, who had served alongside Joshua throughout the conquest, was buried in the hill country of Ephraim.

Three graves. Three testimonies to completed lives. Three witnesses that God's promises had come true.

THE END OF AN ERA

The book closes with a simple but significant statement: "Israel served the LORD throughout the lifetime of Joshua and of the elders who outlived him and who had experienced everything the LORD had done for Israel."

This was the best Israel would ever be. A generation that had seen God's power firsthand, led by a man who had proven himself faithful, living in the land God had promised. They kept their word. They served the Lord.

But the ominous word is "throughout." Throughout Joshua's lifetime. Throughout the lifetime of those elders. What would happen when those leaders were gone? What would happen when the generation that had witnessed the miracles was no longer around to tell the stories? The book of Judges would answer that question—and the answer wouldn't be pretty.

But that's a story for another time. For now, the book of Joshua ends on a note of triumph and faithfulness. Promises made, promises kept. A land given, a people settled. A covenant renewed, a choice declared. "As for me and my household, we will serve the LORD."

TALKING POINTS

Here are some things to think about and discuss:

1. **The eastern tribes were almost destroyed because of a misunderstanding.** What does this story teach us about assuming the worst about people's intentions? How might things have gone differently if the western tribes had attacked without asking questions first?

2. **Joshua told Israel that "not one word" of God's promises had failed.** Looking back through the whole book, what promises do you remember God keeping?

3. **Joshua told the people, "You are not able to serve the LORD."** Why do you think he said this? Was he trying to discourage them or prepare them?

4. **"Choose for yourselves this day whom you will serve."** What does it mean to make this choice in our lives today? What are the "gods" that compete for our attention and loyalty?

5. **The book ends with Israel serving the Lord "throughout the lifetime of Joshua and the elders who outlived him."** Why do you think faithfulness lasted only as long as that generation lived? How do we pass faith to the next generation?

The story of Joshua is complete. A people who had been slaves in Egypt now owned a land flowing with milk and honey. A promise first made to Abraham had finally come true.

But every ending is also a beginning. The question wasn't whether God would keep his promises—he always does. The question was whether Israel would keep theirs.

The choice Joshua presented still echoes today: Whom will you serve? Choose wisely.

www.ingramcontent.com/pod-product-compliance
Ingram Content Group UK Ltd.
Pitfield, Milton Keynes, MK11 3LW, UK
UKHW020420250726
13967UKWH00007B/2738

9 781971 767024